PAUL CÉZANNE

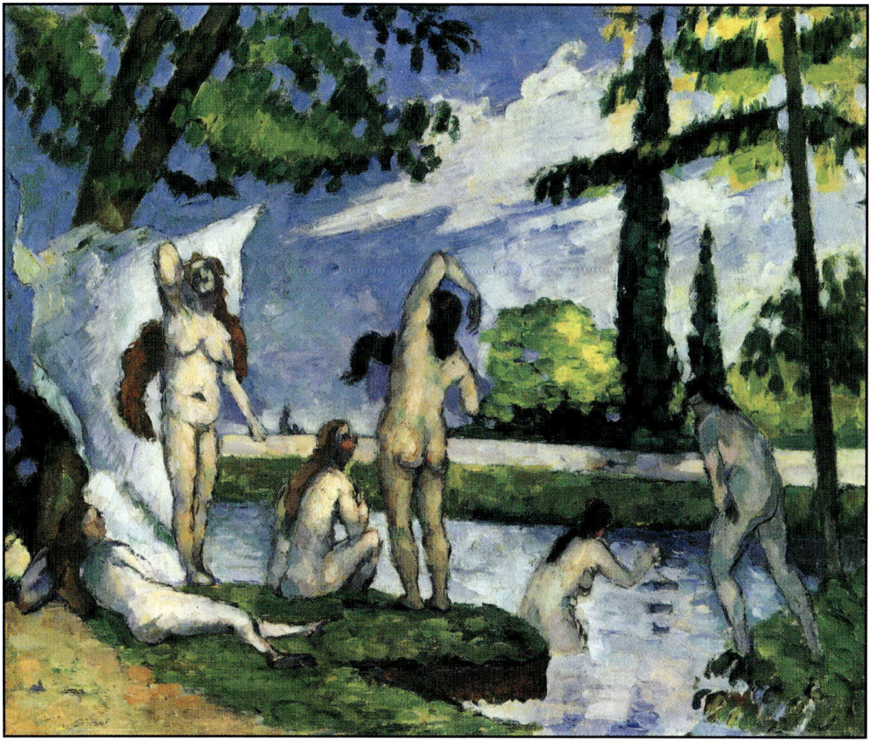

T&J

Published by TAJ Books International LLC 2013
219 Great Lake Drive
Cary, NC 27519
USA
www.tajbooks.com
www.tajminibooks.com

All notations of errors or omissions (author inquiries, permissions) concerning the content of this book should be addressed to info@tajbooks.com.

ISBN 978-1-84406-236-2

Printed in China.
1 2 3 4 5 17 16 15 14 13

PAUL CÉZANNE

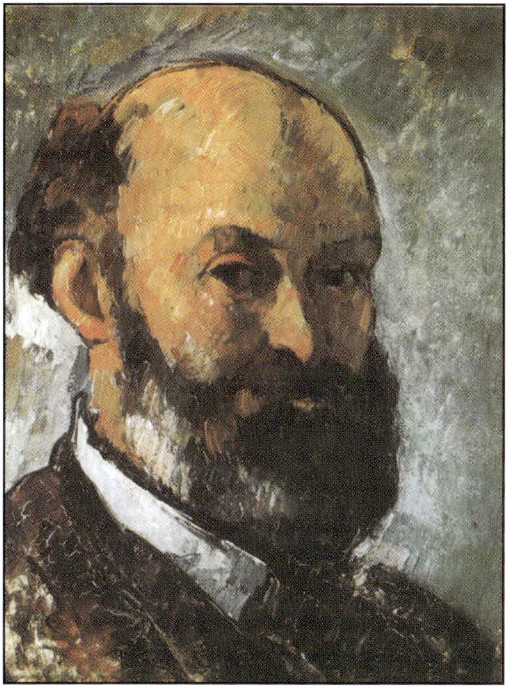

T&J

BY KATHRYN DIXON

PAUL CÉZANNE

1839–1906

Paul Cézanne was a French artist and Post-Impressionist painter whose work was critical in the transition from the 19th-century conception of artistic endeavor to a modern and radically different world of art that emerged full bore in the 20th century. Cézanne and the other Post-Impressionist painters strongly influenced the early-20th-century's new artistic movements of Cubism and Fauvism. Henri Matisse (1869–1954), who is associated with Fauvism, and Pablo Picasso (1881–1973), co-founder of the Cubist movement, are said to have claimed that Cézanne "is the father of us all"—the father of modern art.

One of the most influential artists in the history of 20th-century painting, Cézanne successfully melded the structural impulse of Classicism with the color and emotion of Romanticism, inspiring the generations of artists who followed him to see and portray the world in a more abstract manner. After a brief and unsuccessful sojourn with the Impressionist movement, Cézanne moved away from the realistic portrayal of nature associated with Impressionism. The Impressionists were so named because they strove to capture the fleeting impression of a scene as the forces of nature—light, wind, and so forth—quickly changed its appearance.

Post-Impression—a term selected by the art critic and artist Roger Fry (1866–1934) in order to characterize an exhibition in London's Grafton Galleries in 1910 that introduced the works of the Post-Impressionists to England—is a diverse style of painting in which adherents strive to leave behind the naturalism of Impressionism and to portray instead emotion and symbolism in addition to the visual representation of their subject matter. Post-Impressionism was not a collective movement as was Impressionism, but a group of independent artists; Paul Gauguin (1848–1903), Georges Seurat (1859–1891), and Vincent van Gogh (1853–1890), in addition to Cézanne, are identified with the movement. These four artists were posthumously included in Fry's exhibition, "Manet and the Post-Impressionists." Fry had great aspirations that England would embrace the Post-Impressionists with open arms, but the exhibit was widely panned by the artistic establishment and severely damaged Fry's reputation as a critic.

Cézanne was born in the southern French town of Aix-en-Provence on January 19, 1839. His father was Louis-Auguste Cézanne, a wealthy businessman and banker, and his mother was Anne-Élisabeth-Honorine Auburt, his father's mistress. His parents did not marry until Cézanne was five years old. Cézanne's father, in his mid-forties at the time of his marriage, was a self-made man who engendered envy and scorn as an ascending bourgeois in a small, dull Provençal town. Compounding the resentment surrounding his financial status was his purchase of a 37-acre estate, once belonging to governor of Provence under Louis XIV. This estate,

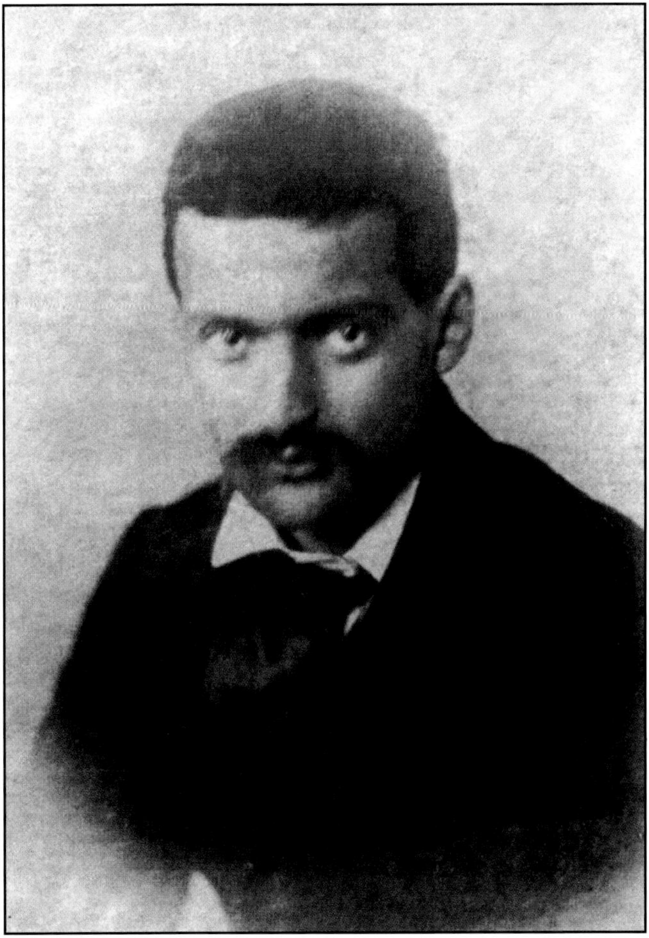

Paul Cézanne, 1861

Jas de Bouffan, was a significant and longstanding influence throughout Cézanne's life—both personal and professional.

Cézanne had two siblings: sisters Marie and Rose. Marie was 2 years his senior and Rose was 15 years his junior. He was as close to Marie as he was distant from Rose, primarily a function of their age difference. Marie would eventually manage Cézanne's finances.

At age 13, Cézanne met his boyhood companion and lifelong champion, Émile Zola (1840–1902)—who would later gain fame as a novelist and man of letters—when they both attended Bourbon College in their hometown of Aix-en-Provence. Zola is the subject of Cézanne's painting, *Paul Alexis Reading to Émile Zola* (1869–70).

Both Zola and Cézanne developed artistic interests at an early age. Cézanne's father was not supportive of his son's choice of profession—having aspirations for his son that reflected his own aggressive self-betterment—but Cézanne persevered and began to paint at the age of 21, in 1860. In 1862, after a number of bitter family disputes, the budding artist was given a small allowance and sent to study art in Paris, where Zola had already preceded him. Zola's letters from Paris did much to encourage Cézanne's desire to follow him there and forge his own career. While in Paris he fought depression and self-doubt and after only six months returned home where he tried for a year to follow in his father's footsteps in banking. The attempt failed miserably and once again he returned to Paris to pursue his dream. For the rest of his life he would move back and forth between Paris and Provence, finding inspiration for his paintings in both places.

Cézanne submitted paintings to the Paris Salon every year from 1865 to 1870, but all were rejected. Tortured by his conflicting desires for acceptance and fame and for rebellion, Cézanne staggered between inspiration and depression, disappearing for weeks at a time away from public discourse. When the professional strains in Paris became too overwhelming, Cézanne would go home to Aix, returning to Paris when he was more able to cope. Throughout his professional career, he would paint most often at the family estate of Jas de Bouffan.

In Paris, while attending the art school Académie Suisse in 1869, Cézanne met his future wife, Marie-Hortense Fiquet, who worked as a bookbinder. She was 11 years younger than the artist. As his mistress, Marie-Hortense was Cézanne's first steady romantic female relationship and would also be his last. Although they were apart many of their 40 years together, neither pursued other romantic relationships. In 1870, at the outbreak of the Franco-Prussian War, the couple left Paris for the French seaside town of L'Estaque, where his mother owned a small vacation house, near Marseilles. Their only child, Paul, was born two years later in 1872. Fearing the loss of his allowance, Cézanne kept his son's birth a secret from his father for a number of years.

Cézanne's early paintings, which combine romantic and classical themes, are imbued with dark colors and executed with an expressive brushwork in the tradition of Delacroix. Dramatic tonal contrasts and thick layers of pigment (often applied with a palette knife) exemplify the vigor in which Cézanne painted during the 1860s, especially apparent in the portrait series of his maternal uncle, Dominique Aubert, variously costumed as a lawyer, an artist, and a monk. This kind of costume piece is reminiscent of Manet's Spanish paintings of the 1860s.

Many of Cézanne's early works were painted in dark tones applied with heavy, fluid pigment, suggesting the moody, romantic expressionism of previous generations. Just as Zola pursued his interest in the realist novel, Cézanne also gradually developed a commitment to the representation of contemporary life, painting the world he observed with an emphasis on its governing structure (i.e., the reality that underlay the visual impression).

The most significant influence on the work of his early maturity proved to be Camille Pissarro (1830–1903), an older but as yet unrecognized painter who lived with his large family in the rural town of Pontoise outside Paris. The moody and socially uneasy Cézanne, distanced from most of his Parisian friends as well as from his father, who was still uninformed about Marie-Hortense, welcomed an invitation from Pissarro for his family (including his newly born son) to join Pissarro's family at their home in 1872. Pissarro provided the moral encouragement that the insecure Cézanne sought.

Along with the painters Claude Monet (1840–1926), Auguste Renoir (1841–1919), and a few others, Pissarro developed a painting style that involved working outdoors (*en plein air*) rapidly and on a reduced scale, employing small touches of pure color, generally without the use of preparatory sketches or linear outlines. At this time, plein-air painting was considered a radical departure from tradition. Leaving the studio to work outdoors was until this time almost unheard of. By painting in the very midst of the scene itself, Pissarro and the others hoped to capture the most transient of natural effects as well as their own passing emotional states. Under Pissarro's guidance, and within a very short time in the years 1872 and 1873, Cézanne shifted from dark tones to bright hues and began to concentrate on scenes of farmland and rural villages. With this change of direction, Cézanne entered his short-lived Impressionist phase.

Although somewhat less technically accomplished than the other artists who were embracing the new Impressionist techniques, Cézanne was half-heartedly accepted by the group—named the Batignolles group after the Paris quarter in which the Café Guerbois, which most of them frequented, was located—and exhibited with them in 1874 and 1877. Chief among the Batignolles painters, soon to be known as the Impressionists, was Édouard Manet, the group's intellectual leader, as well as Edgar Degas, Claude Monet, Camille Pissarro, Pierre-Auguste Renoir, Armand Guillaumin, and Alfred Sisley. When Cézanne showed up at the Café Gerbois he remained broodingly aloof from the social banter and artistic argument, much less accepting of the group than they of him.

In fact, in spring 1874, as the Impressionists were readying their first public exhibition, many wanted to exclude the unconventional Cézanne, concerned that his inclusion would further distance the group from public acceptance. Pissarro argued vehemently against ostracizing Cézanne, and Cézanne was allowed to hang three works: *Modern Olympia* (the second painting by that name), an unnamed landscape, and *The House of the Hanged Man*. This last painting is considered to be Cézanne's first Impressionist work. For a while after the painting was completed, Cézanne adopted a small drawing of a hanged man as a sort of logo or signature in the corner of his paintings. As anticipated, Cézanne did draw the public's and the critics' wrath, in particular with his erotic and boldly conceived painting, *A Modern Olympia*, a satire of Édouard Manet's even more notorious *Olympia*.

Cézanne did not participate in the 1876 Impressionist exhibition, but did submit 16 works (3 watercolors and 13 oils) for the third group exhibition in 1877. One of the oils, *The Bathers*, which was painted in 1874–75, was one of his first paintings on this theme; others followed, painted over the next 30 years. The landscape of *The Bathers* has the brilliance of plein-air painting, but the figures were drawn from the artist's imagination; Cézanne rarely painted nudes from life. The challenge of melding these two disparate sources—nature and memory—would be a theme of Cézanne's work for years to come.

In general, the Impressionists did not have commercial success, and Cézanne's works received the harshest critical commentary. One Belgian critic said of his work that it was little more than "sincere daubing." Another critic wrote that "when children amuse themselves with paints and paper they do better" than Cézanne. Disappointed and disillusioned, he drifted away from many of his Parisian contemporaries during the late 1870s and 1880s and began to spend much of his time in his native Aix. After 1882, he did not work closely again with Pissarro. From this point forward, Cézanne is typically characterized as a Post-Impressionist, building form with color, albeit using the techniques of the Impressionists such as "broken color" (i.e., using unmixed brightly colored pigments layered on in short brushstrokes), but undertaken with his own modifications.

After years of struggling in obscurity, Zola was the first of the two friends to achieve a measure of success and notoriety with the publication of his novel *L'Assommoir*. Literary critics and the public alike—regardless of the fact that the book sold over 100,000 copies in only a few months—were shocked with Zola's naturalistic style. The sequel, *Nana*, drew even more scornful commentary, yet was a tremendous financial success.

In 1885, disgusted by what he perceived as Zola's bourgeois lifestyle, Cézanne broke off relations with his oldest supporter. He would never see his old friend again. The next year, 1886,

Cézanne inherited his father's wealth, and finally, at the age of 47 became financially independent, but he remained socially quite isolated.

Fiquet and Cézanne finally married in 1886 after his father's death, although by that time Cézanne claimed to have lost all feelings for her. Afterward, he and Fiquet lived separately. Cézanne moved into the family home, Jas de Bouffan, in Aix where he lived with his mother and his sister Marie. Neither mother nor sister accepted Fiquet, whom Cézanne's friends nicknamed "La Boule" (The Ball), as in ball and chain, because of her doggedly bourgeois outlook and her ability to spend frivolously all money that Cézanne bestowed upon her. Cézanne disinherited Fiquet and left all of his estate, inherited from his own father, to his son, Paul. Although emotionally estranged and living apart for the majority of their marriage, Cézanne continued to paint his dark-haired wife. More than 40 paintings of Madame Cézanne populate his body of work. Given Cézanne's style, none is an exact likeness, although the conclusion can be drawn that she was not a beauty.

Cézanne's goal was, in his own mind, never fully attained. He left most of his works unfinished and destroyed many others. History can thank Julien Tanguy, a Parisian paint dealer, for persuading Cézanne not to destroy many of the paintings he disliked. Tanguy bartered with some of the best known artists of the era to exchange their painted canvases for paints. In this way, he collected numerous works of Cézanne, Pissarro, Gauguin, van Gogh, Sisley, Seurat, and many others.

An even earlier patron of Cézanne was Dr. Paul-Ferdinand Gachet of Pontoise, the town in which Pissarro lived and Cézanne visited. Over 50 years, Dr. Gachet accepted paintings from a number of artists in lieu of payment for medical services as well as purchased them outright. An amateur painter, he had an exceptionally keen eye for talent, encouraging other businessmen around Pontoise to accept payment in the form of painted canvases. Dr. Gachet was the first to purchase a painting from Cézanne–the second version of *A Modern Olympia*, which was shown in 1874 in Paris at the first Impressionist exhibition and caused such an uproar that Cézanne's reputation as an artist was sullied for much of the remainder of his life.

A third supporter of Cézanne was Victor Chocquet. Chocquet was a customs official who, although not wealthy, was a major collector of the new Impressionists. Upon seeing one of the paintings in Cézanne's *Bathers* series, he immediately purchased it. Chocquet's introduction to Cézanne is variously attributed to Julien Tanguy and to Renoir. Two versions of a *Portrait of Victor Chocquet*–one of them a full-body study with Chocquet seated–were executed by Cézanne around 1877. At the time of his death, Chocquet owned more than 30 paintings by Cézanne.

From 1882 to 1885, Cézanne lived primarily in Provence, executing a large number of landscape pictures of his native Aix and of L'Estaque, the small fishing village to which he originally escaped from

Paris 12 years earlier at the outset of the Franco-Prussian War with his then-mistress Marie-Hortense. He made an unexpected return to Paris in 1883 to attend Manet's funeral, also attended by Renoir, Pissarro, Zola, Degas, and Monet.

Unusual for an artist, Cézanne rotated his attention relatively equally throughout his career among portrait painting, figure painting, still lifes, and landscapes. Around the time of Manet's death, however, Cézanne had turned his focus to still lifes, beginning an exploration of the style and following in the footsteps of his contemporary, Manet. Over three decades, Cézanne's still lifes evolved from the conventional approach of the 18th century of a very linear perspective to a more distorted, fluid perspective and intricate composition for which he used muted tones in a palette revised from his Impressionist days.

As with all things, Cézanne adopted his own approach to painting a still life. Contrary to his predecessors, he made no effort to hide the fabrications he concocted to create the image he wanted to portray. *Still Life with a Basket of Apples* (1895) clearly shows a block of wood on which the basket is leaning. *Still Life: Apples and a Pot of Primroses* (1890–1894) reveals Cézanne's mastery of building forms with color and of devising compositions using distorted perspectival space. Cézanne gave precedence to the relationship of one object to another in lieu of the traditional single-point perspective typical of Classicism.

Fruit, in particular apples, and the basic, simple accoutrements of daily life such as a bottle, bowl, or dish were common subjects of Cézanne's still lifes rather than the elegant jewelry, complex fabric textures, or delicate porcelain, which were the traditional subjects of his predecessors. Many of his still lifes contain optical contradictions and distortions such as *Still Life with Fruit Basket* (1888–1890), which portrays the table top on a different plane on either side of the napkin draped over the table. Cézanne's interest in the still life, in contrast to the 19th-century painters' focus on the landscape, was a precursor to the emphasis on still lifes as painted by the Cubists and other modern artists.

Cézanne worked incessantly on his canvases, often giving up in disgust if he was unhappy with the result. One story tells of Renoir finding a watercolor in the *Bathers* series discarded among the rocks in the hills above L'Estaque when he was visiting Cézanne. Cézanne admitted to nearly 20 sessions with the painting before he tossed it aside. Another example of his dogged determination to execute his vision is *Still Life: Vase with Flowers* (1903) on which he worked for over a year, yet still viewed by him as unfinished.

The landscapes of Cézanne emphasize the structure and form of nature and its elements' relationships in space, while de-emphasizing the more minor details of the scene. In *Orchard in Pontoise* (1877), Cézanne almost eliminates the trees in the orchard in the forefront of the painting to build the form of the houses with their blue-hued

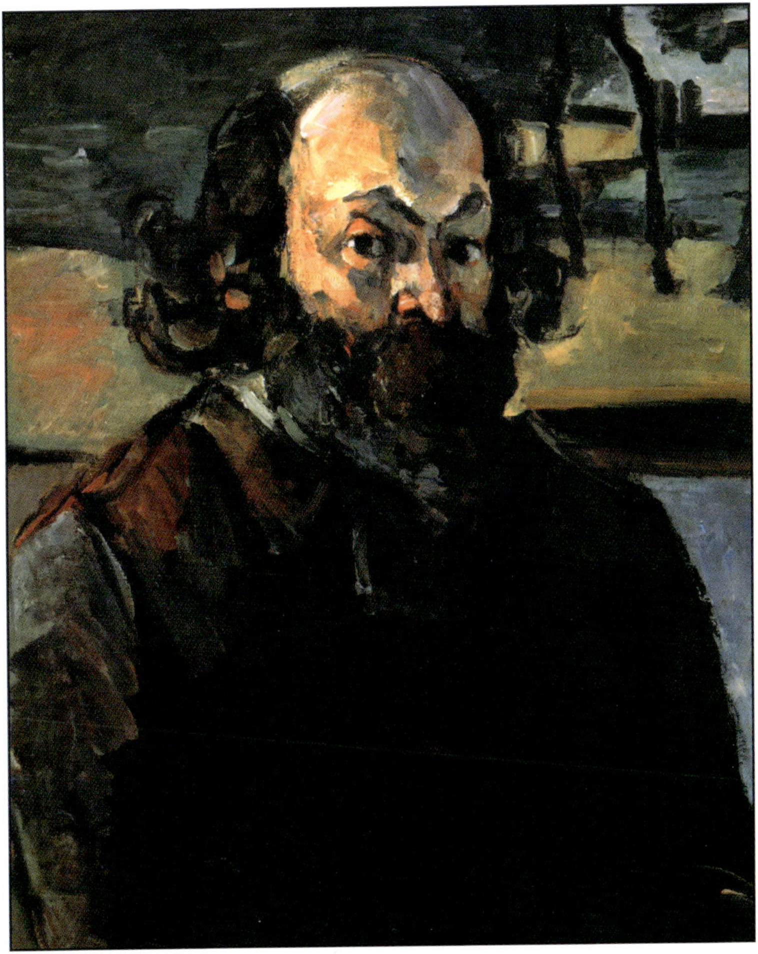

Self-Portrait

roofs and shutters in the background. Cézanne uses the application and layering of color in order to delineate form instead of achieving the same through drawing or outlining, offering the essence of the landscape without its intricate detail. Near the end of his life, Cézanne took his evolution toward abstraction to an even higher pitch with his watercolor, *Mont Sainte-Victoire* (1904–1906), in which the three-dimensional aspect of conventional landscapes is dismissed in favor of glorious color and the energy of brushstrokes to evoke the forest, desert, mountain, and sky beyond.

Cézanne was never interested in fantastical or unrealistic depictions of his subjects, even if spatial relationships were sometimes slightly distorted. Yet the method, known as "flat depth," that Cézanne adopted for his landscapes as he matured professionally is a concerted effort to call attention to the fact that his depiction of nature is, in fact, a painting, a vision, an interpretation. *Monte Sainte-Victoire as Seen from Bibémus Quarry* (1898–1900) is an excellent example of flat depth, grown even flatter than in his earlier landscapes, such as *House in Provence* (1882–1885). In order to create the aspect of depth in flat depth, Cézanne used a technique that he called "modulating," that is, alternating warm and cool colors to define advancing and receding surfaces. Modulation was used to great effect in *Rocks at Fontainebleau* (1894–1898).

In 1890, Cézanne began painting a series of five pictures—varied in the number of players and onlookers—of Provençal peasants playing cards. Widely celebrated as among the finest figure compositions completed by the artist, the series *The Card Players* demonstrates Cézanne's system of color gradations to build form and create a three-dimensional quality in the figures.

In 1895, after nearly two decades in which Cézanne's work was absent from Paris, Ambroise Vollard (1867–1939), a Paris art dealer, arranged at his gallery the first one-man show of Cézanne's works. He was encouraged to do so by Cézanne's old Batignolles contemporaries, chiefly Pissarro. Over the next few years, Vollard promoted Cézanne quite successfully. Although the exhibition met with some skepticism, Cézanne's reputation as a great artist grew, and he was finally discussed and promoted by a small circle of enthusiasts, including the art historian and critic Bernard Berenson, American painter Mary Cassatt (1844–1926), and the American art collectors Henry Osborne Havemeyer and his wife Louisine Havemeyer, a friend of Mary Cassatt. Posthumous exhibitions at Galerie Bernheim-Jeune, where 79 watercolors were exhibited, and the Salon d'Automne, where 48 canvases were shown, in 1907 in Paris established Cézanne's artistic legacy even before the infamous Post-Impressionist exhibition of Roger Fry in 1910 in London.

From about the mid-1890s, many younger artists traveled to Aix to observe Cézanne at work and to receive any words of wisdom he might offer. Both his style and his theory remained unconventional and cryptic, yet the intensity of his color, coupled with the rigor of his compositional organization, signaled that Cézanne had quite successfully synthesized the basic expressive and representational elements of painting in a highly original manner. Cézanne's advice to his young admirers was to engage in their own artistic endeavor to find their own unique style rather than to replicate his.

For many years of his life, Cézanne was known and appreciated primarily by his old Impressionist colleagues and to the other artists—van Gogh, Gauguin, and Seurat—who are known now as the Post-Impressionists. Sadly, Cézanne's art was misunderstood and discredited by the public during most of his life. In time, he was able to successfully challenge all of the conventional values of 19th-century painting to father the more modern and radical movements of Fauvism, Cubism, and Abstract Expressionists, which were to turn the art world of the 20th century on its head.

Cézanne gained the recognition he sought in his lifetime when his painting, *Boy in a Red Vest* (1889–1895), sold in 1958 at auction to the American banker Paul Mellon for the then-unprecedented sum of $616,000. The innovative artist has continued to enthrall art collectors and the public in the ensuing years. In February 2012, the royal family of Qatar paid the highest price ever for a work of art—£160 million ($250 million)—for one painting in the series *The Card Players*.

Cézanne's work demonstrates a timeless mastery of design, color, and composition. In total, Cézanne's lifetime body of work includes well over 700 works. His often repetitive brushstrokes are highly characteristic of his methods and clearly recognizable as his creative genius. He used planes of color and small brushstrokes to form complex fields, both a direct expression of the sensations of the observing eye and an abstraction from observed nature. The paintings convey Cézanne's intense study of his subjects and a determined struggle to deal with the complexity of human visual perception. Lamenting late in life that he was unable to realize his vision, he wrote that "[o]ld age and failing health will see to it now that the dream of art I have spent my life pursuing will never come true."

On October 22, 1906, after collapsing on October 15, bombarded by a rainstorm on his almost daily walk to paint the countryside near Aix, and then catching pneumonia complicated by diabetes, Cézanne died at his apartment on Rue Boulegon attended only by his sister, Marie. She had summoned his wife and son Paul from Paris to be with him at the end, but they arrived too late. It is said that in his last hours he was tortured by one of the greatest disappointments of his life: the refusal of Auguste-Henri Pontier, the director of the Musée Granet in Aix, to accept his works. Pontier had vowed that while he was alive he would allow no painting of Cézanne to hang in the museum. It appears that Cézanne had the last laugh.

Plate 1

THE KISS OF THE MUSE

1860, Musée d'Orsay, Paris
82 x 66 cm

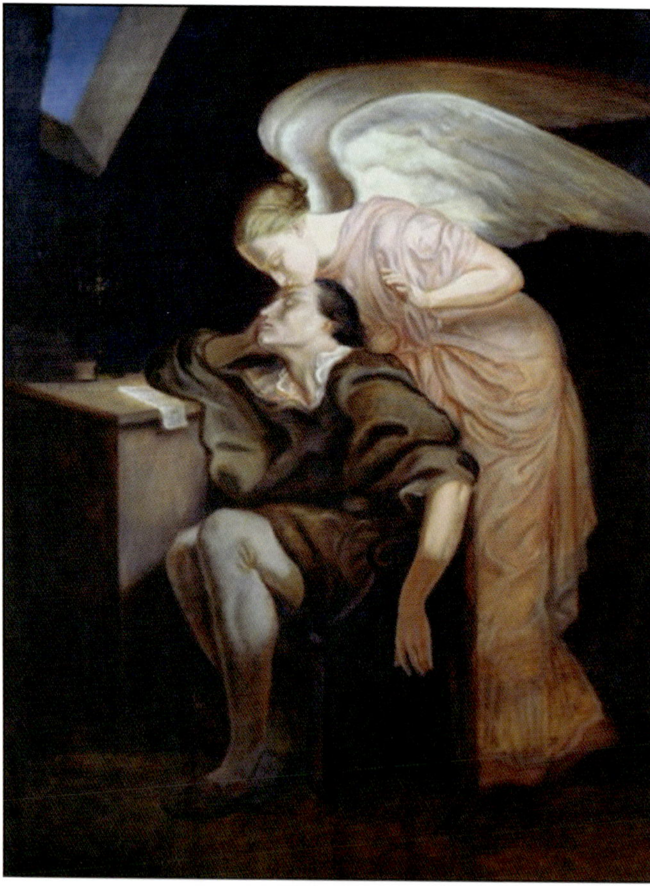

Plate 2

FATHER OF THE ARTIST LOUIS-AUGUSTE CÉZANNE

1865, National Gallery, London
167.6 x 114.3 cm

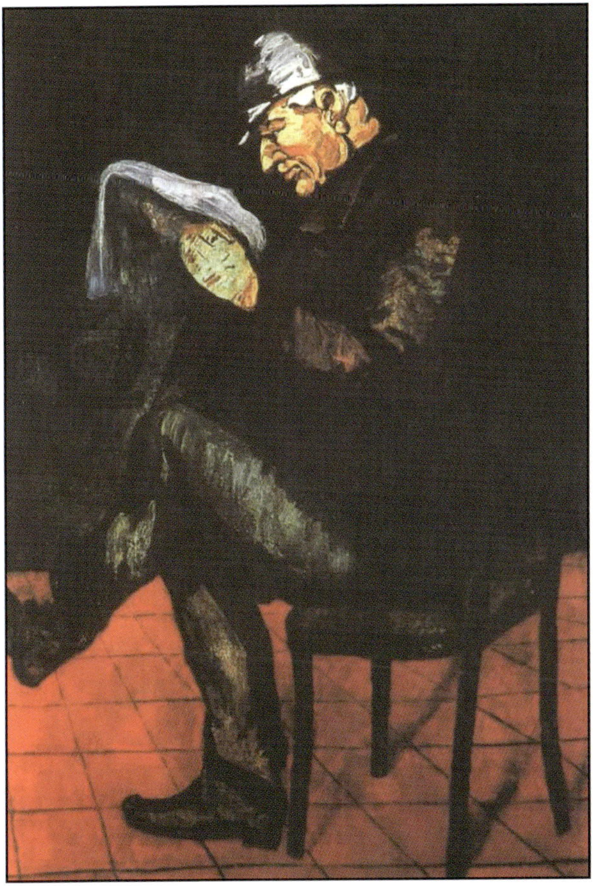

Plate 3

STILL LIFE WITH BREAD AND EGGS

1865, Cincinnati Art Museum, Ohio
59 x 76 cm

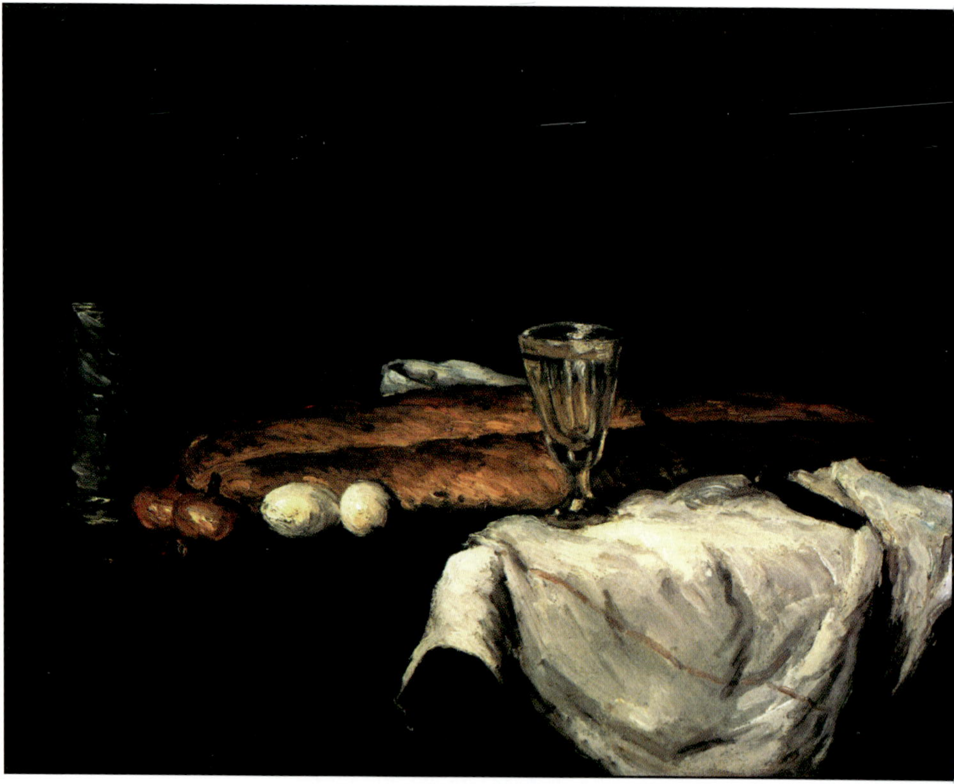

HEAD OF AN OLD MAN

1866, Musée d'Orsay, Paris
51 x 48 cm

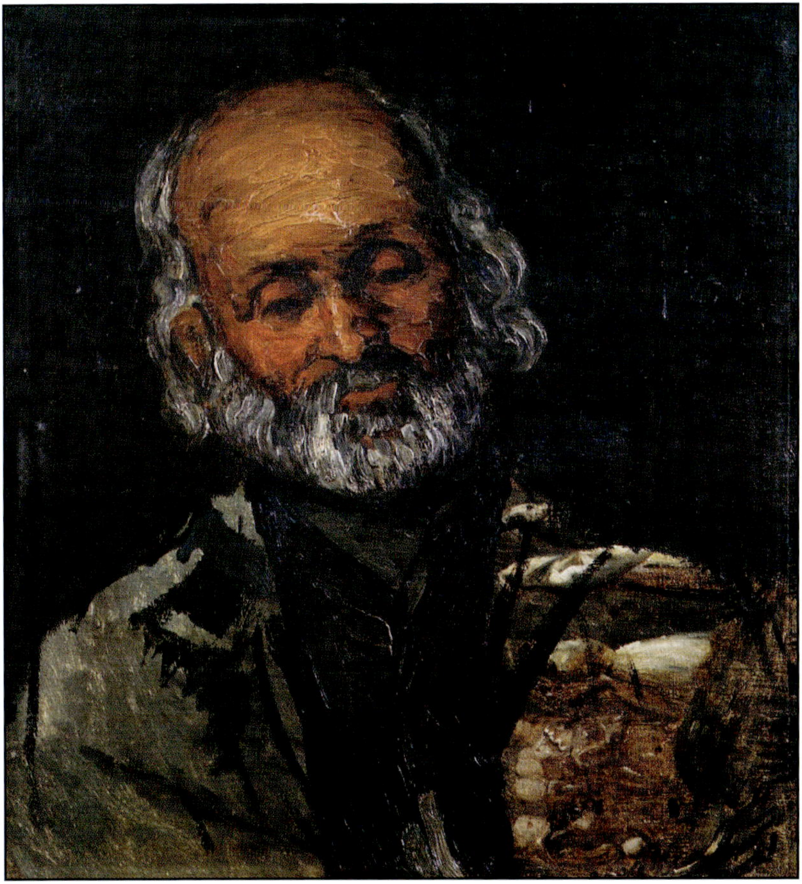

Plate 5

THE ARTIST'S FATHER READING HIS NEWSPAPER

1866, National Gallery of Art, Washington, DC
198.5 x 119.3 cm

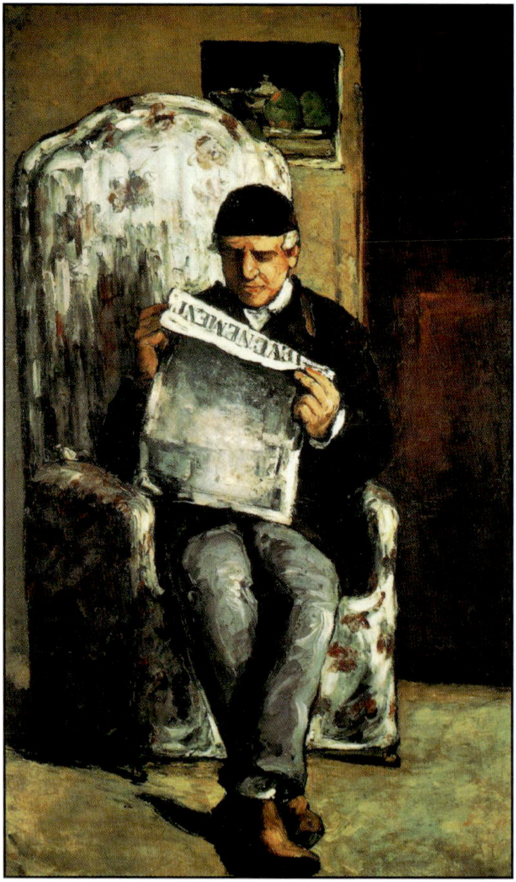

THE LION AND THE BASIN AT JAS DE BOUFFAN

1866, Musée d'Orsay, Paris
46 x 60.5 cm

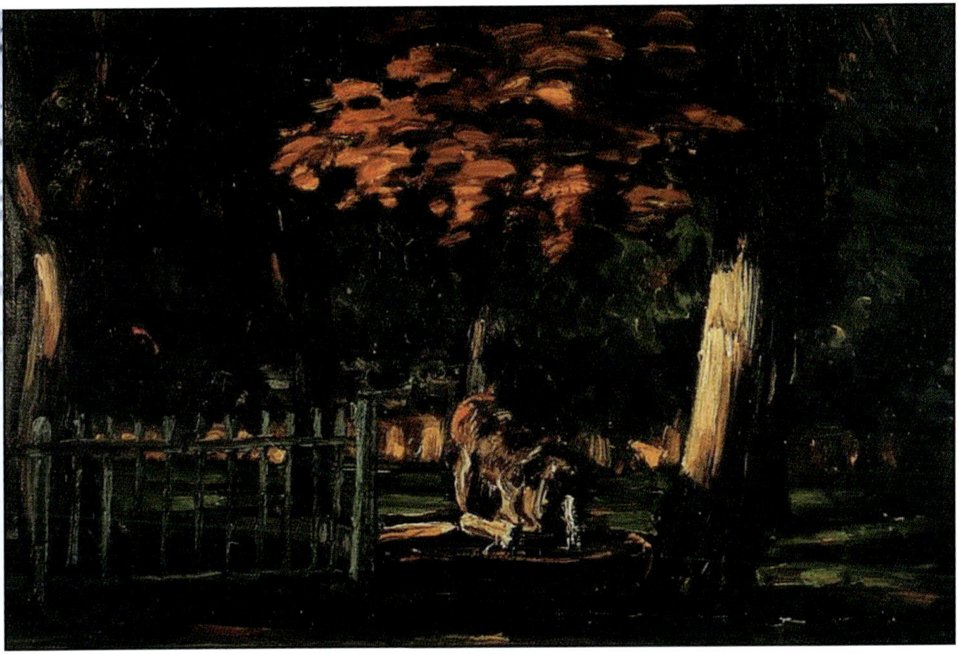

Plate 7 PORTRAIT OF UNCLE DOMINIQUE AS A MONK

1866, Metropolitan Museum of Art, New York City
64.8 x 54 cm

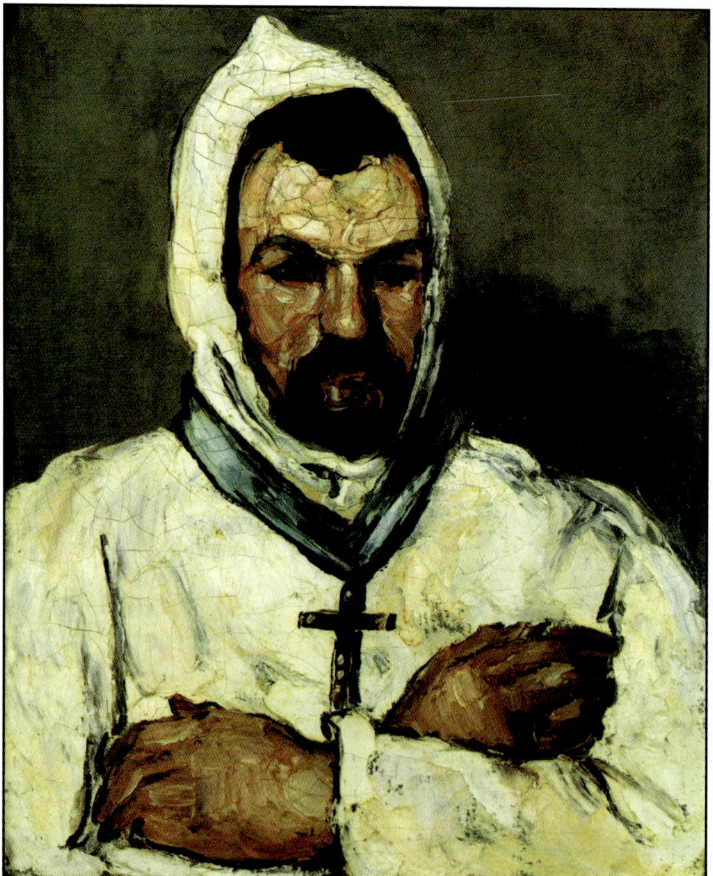

ANTOINE DOMINIQUE SAUVEUR AUBERT

1866, Metropolitan Museum of Art, New York City
80 x 65 cm

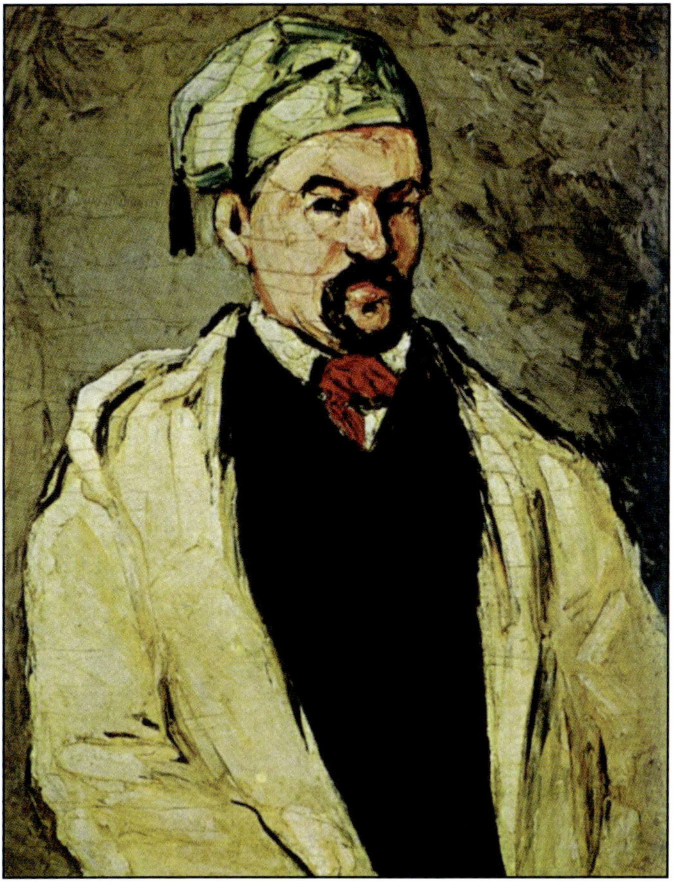

SORROW

1867, Musée d'Orsay, Paris
168 x 126.4 cm

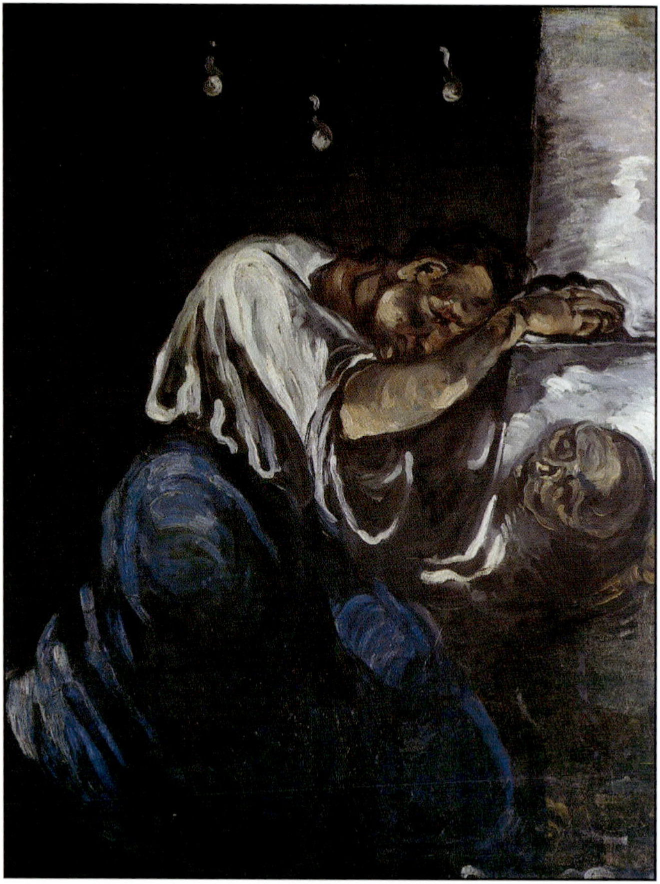

THE ABDUCTION

1867, Fitzwilliam Museum, Cambridge, UK
90.5 x 117 cm

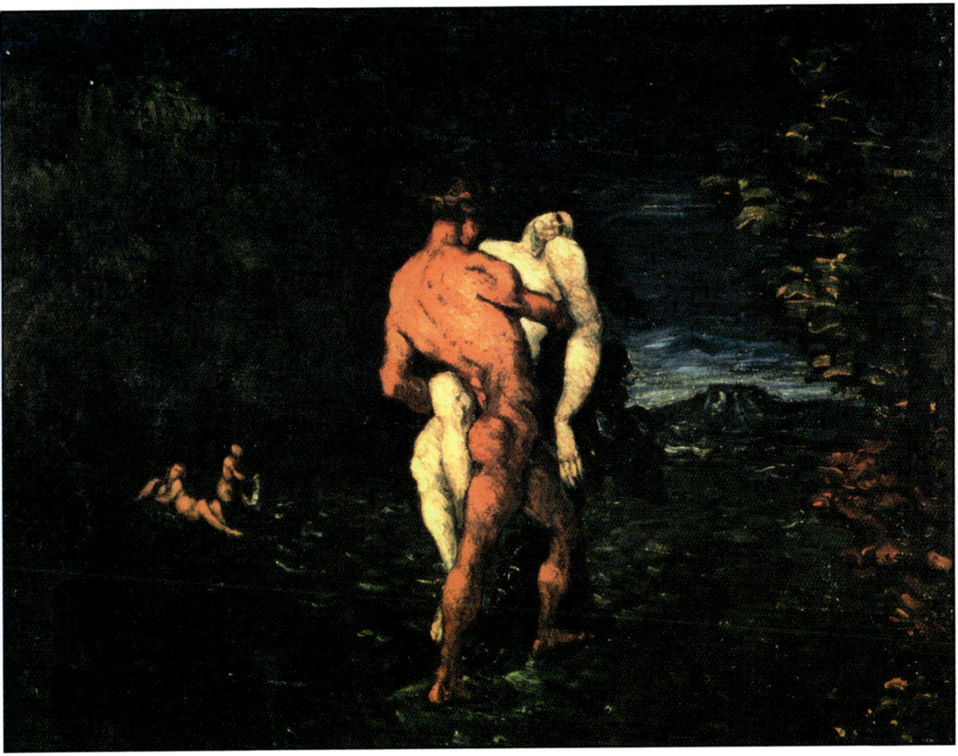

Plate 11

THE MURDER

1868, Walker Art Gallery, Liverpool, UK
65.5 x 80.7 cm

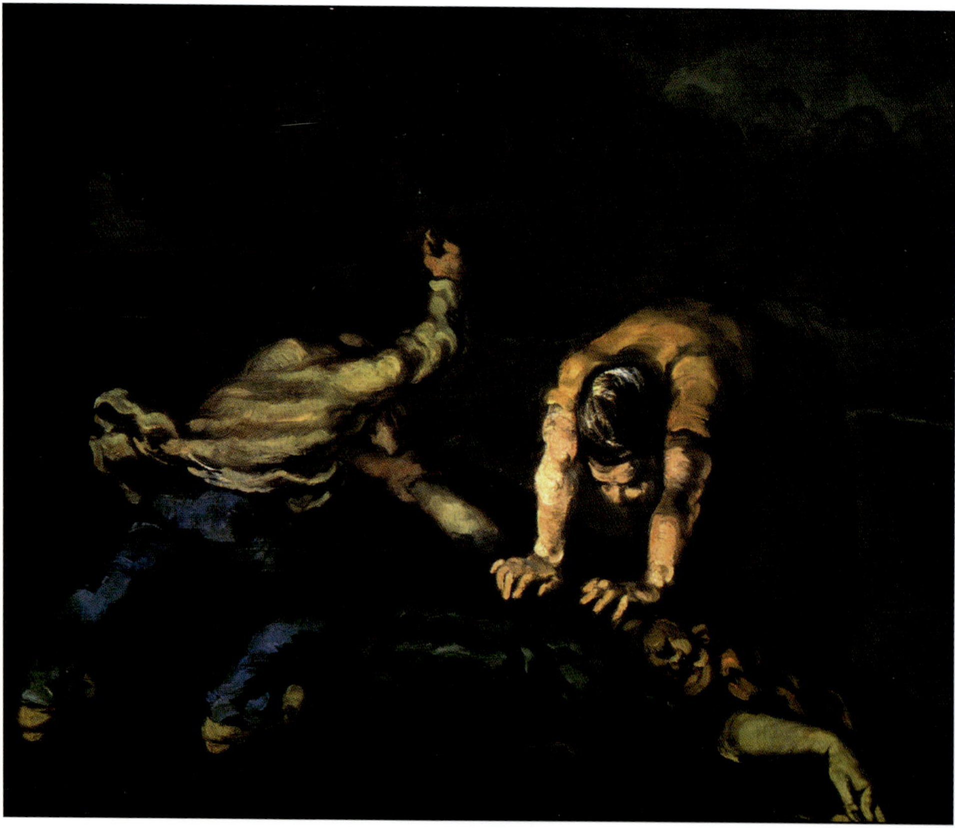

GIRL AT THE PIANO

1869, The State Hermitage Museum, St. Petersburg, Russia
57 x 92 cm

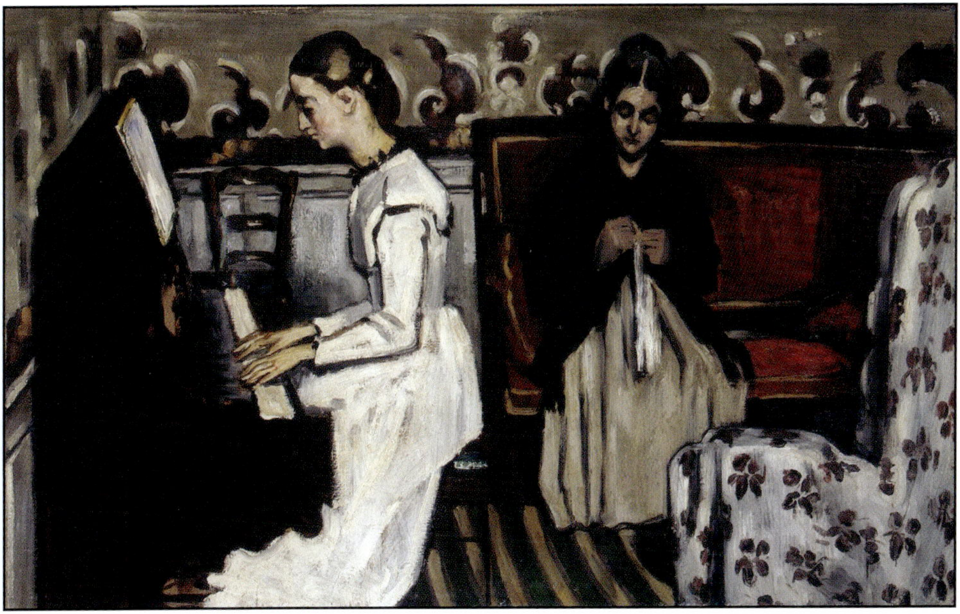

PAUL ALEXIS READING A MANUSCRIPT TO ÉMILE ZOLA

1870, Museu de Arte, Sao Paulo, Brazil
130 x 160 cm

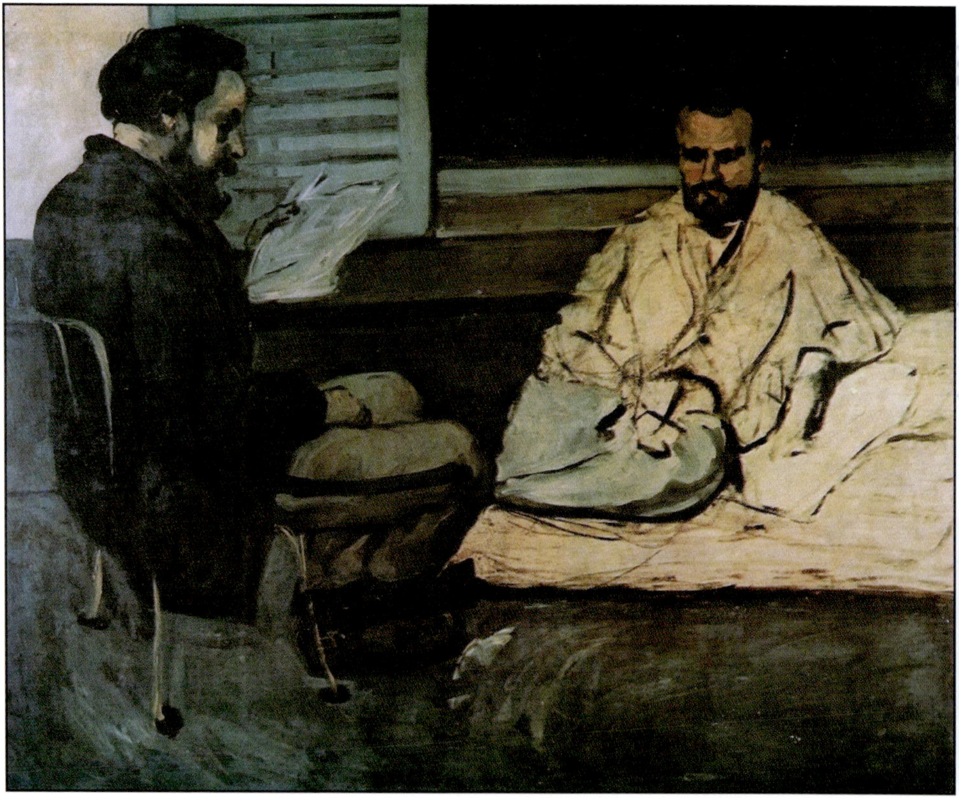

PORTRAIT OF ANTHONY VALABRÈGUE

1870, The J. Paul Getty Museum, Los Angeles
60.4 x 50.2 cm

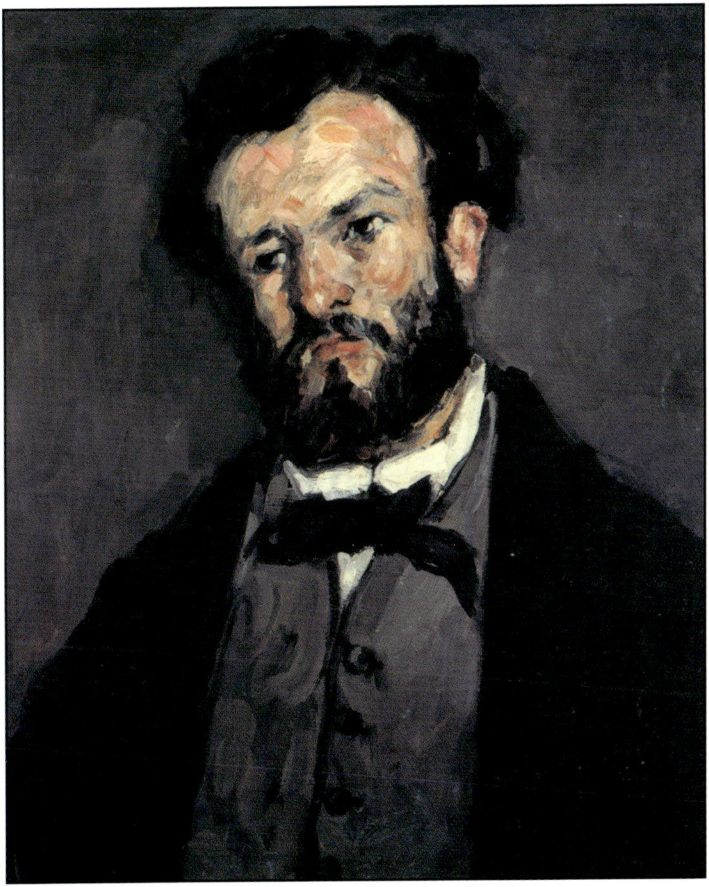

PASTORAL

1870, Musée d'Orsay, Paris
65 x 81 cm

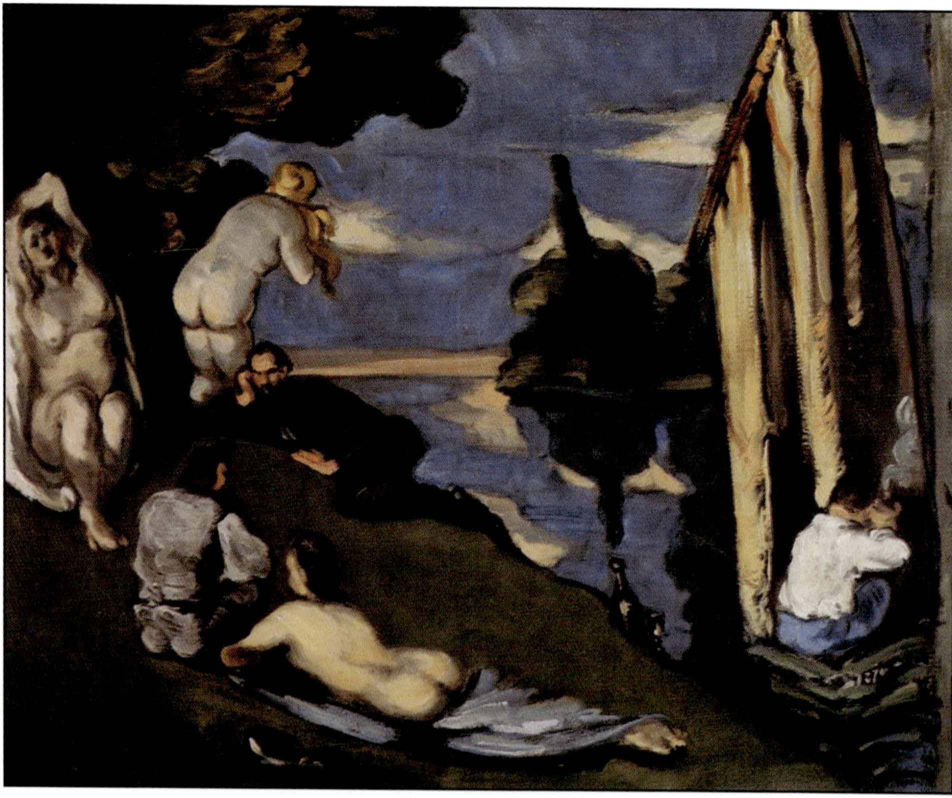

STILL LIFE WITH GREEN POT AND PEWTER JUG

1870, Musée d'Orsay, Paris
64.5 x 81 cm

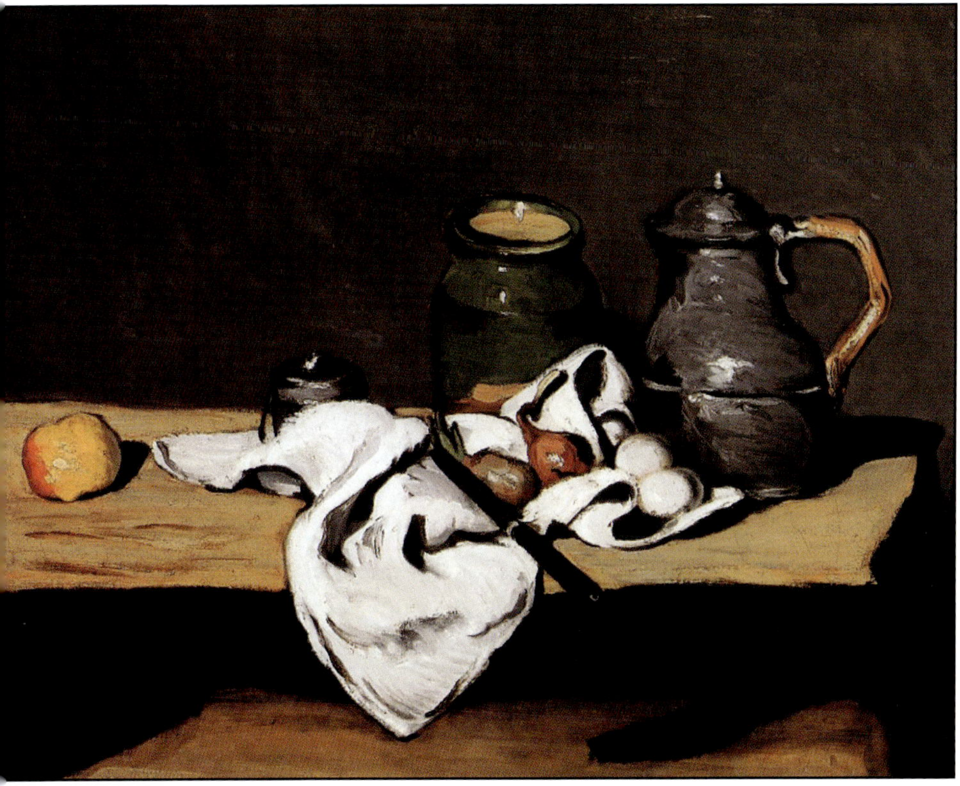

Plate 17

THE RAILWAY CUTTING

1870, Neue Pinakothek, Munich
80 x 129 cm

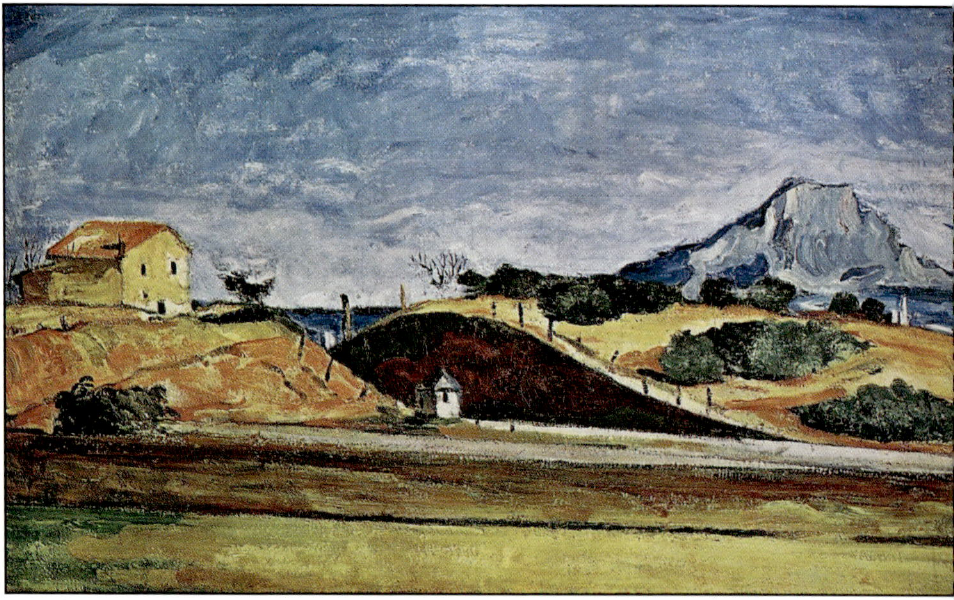

GUSTAVE BOYER IN A STRAW HAT

1871, Metropolitan Museum of Art, New York City
55 x 39 cm

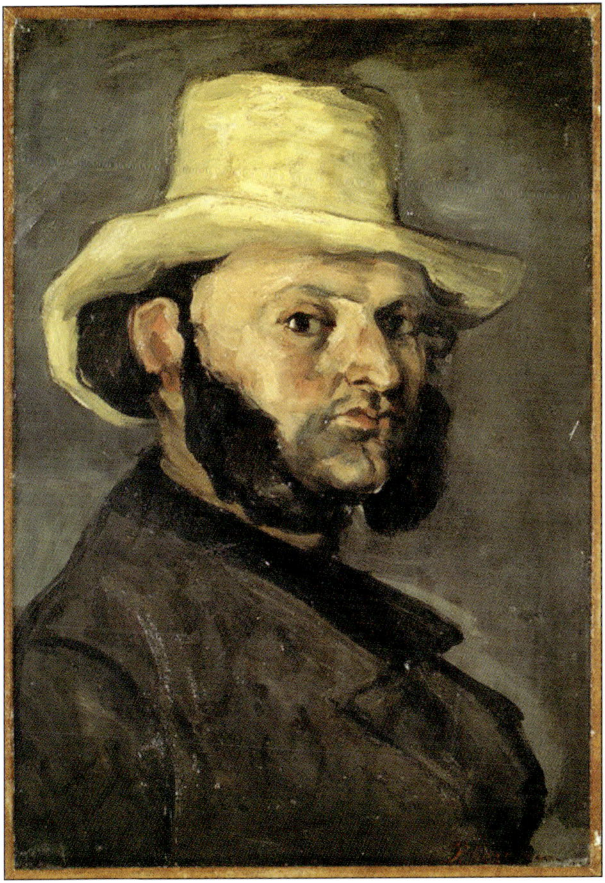

Plate 19

THE HANGED MAN'S HOUSE IN AUVERS

1873, Musée d'Orsay, Paris
21 x 26 cm

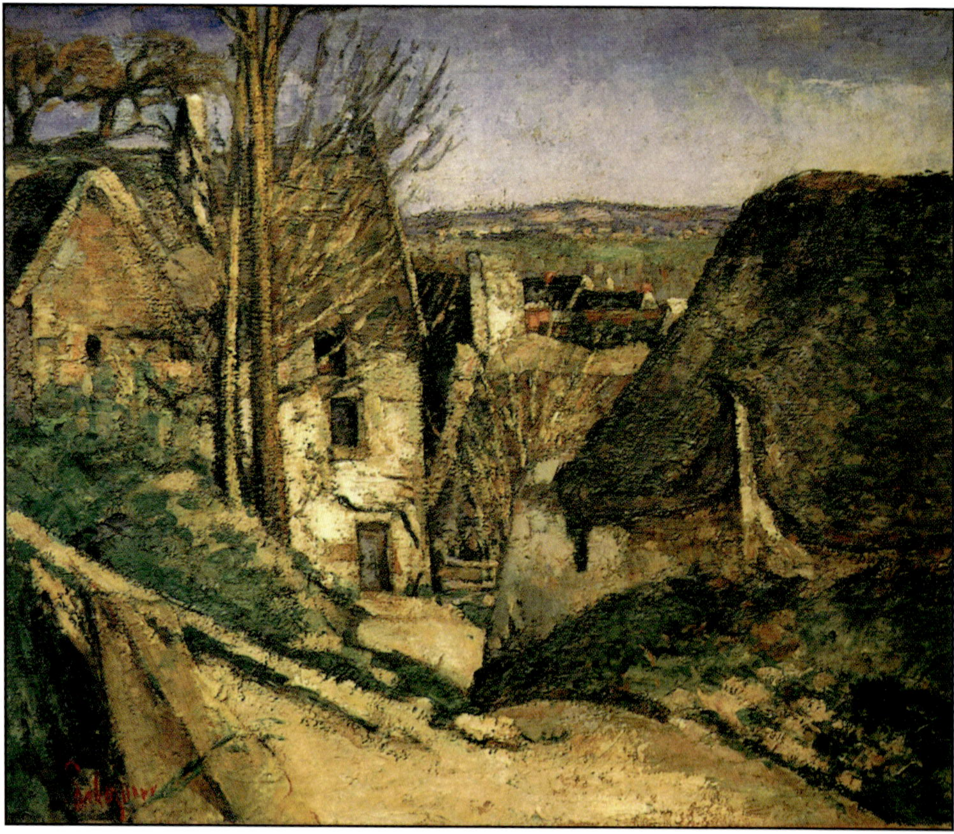

THE HOUSE OF PERE LACROIX IN AUVERS

1873, National Gallery of Art, Washington, DC
61.5 x 51 cm

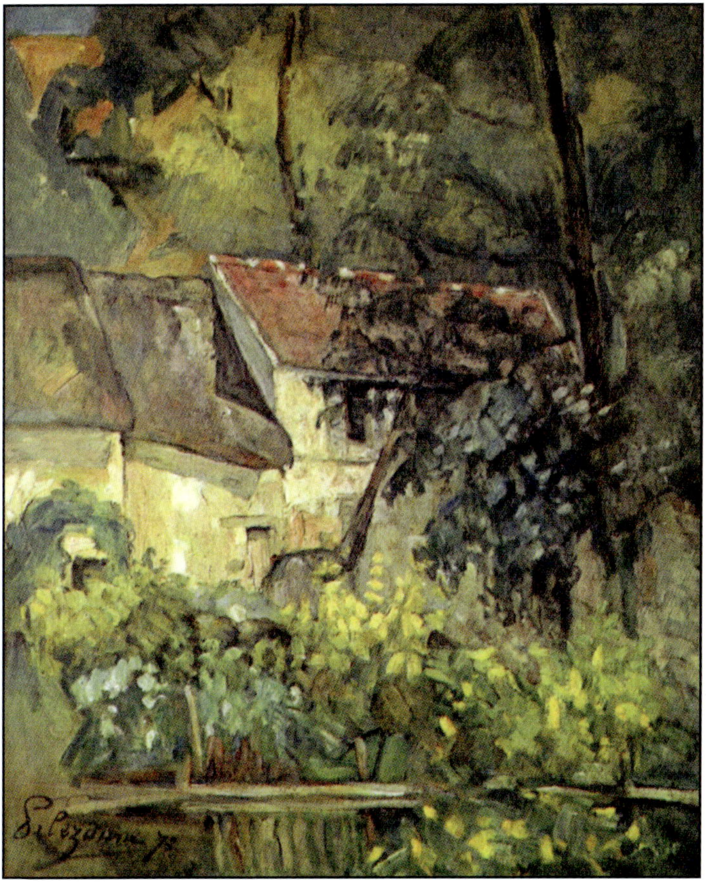

Plate 21

VIEW OF AUVERS

1873, Art Institute of Chicago
65 x 80 cm

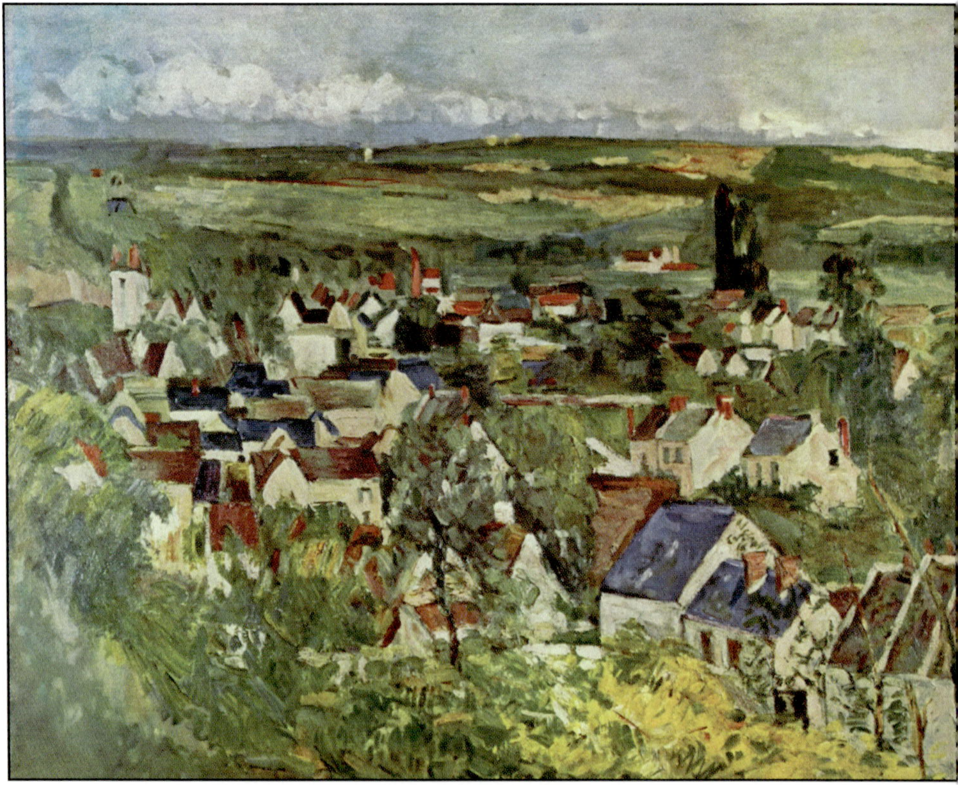

BATHERS

1875, Metropolitan Museum of Art, New York City
38.1 x 46 cm

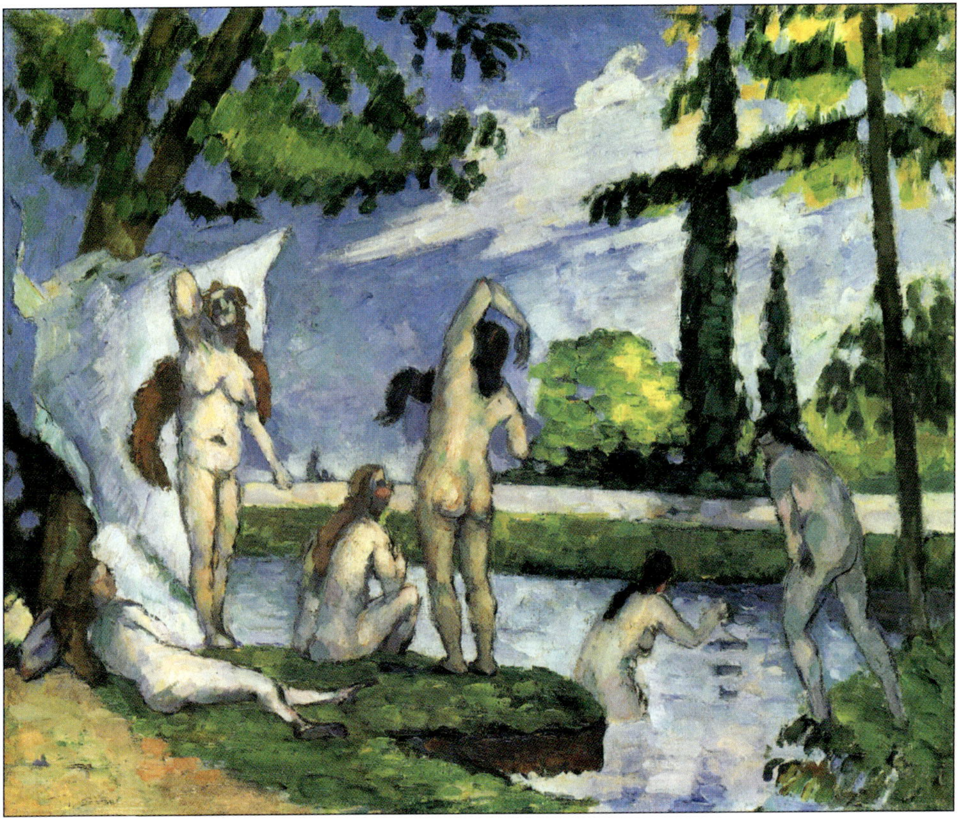

A MODERN OLYMPIA

1874, Musée d'Orsay, Paris
46 x 55 cm

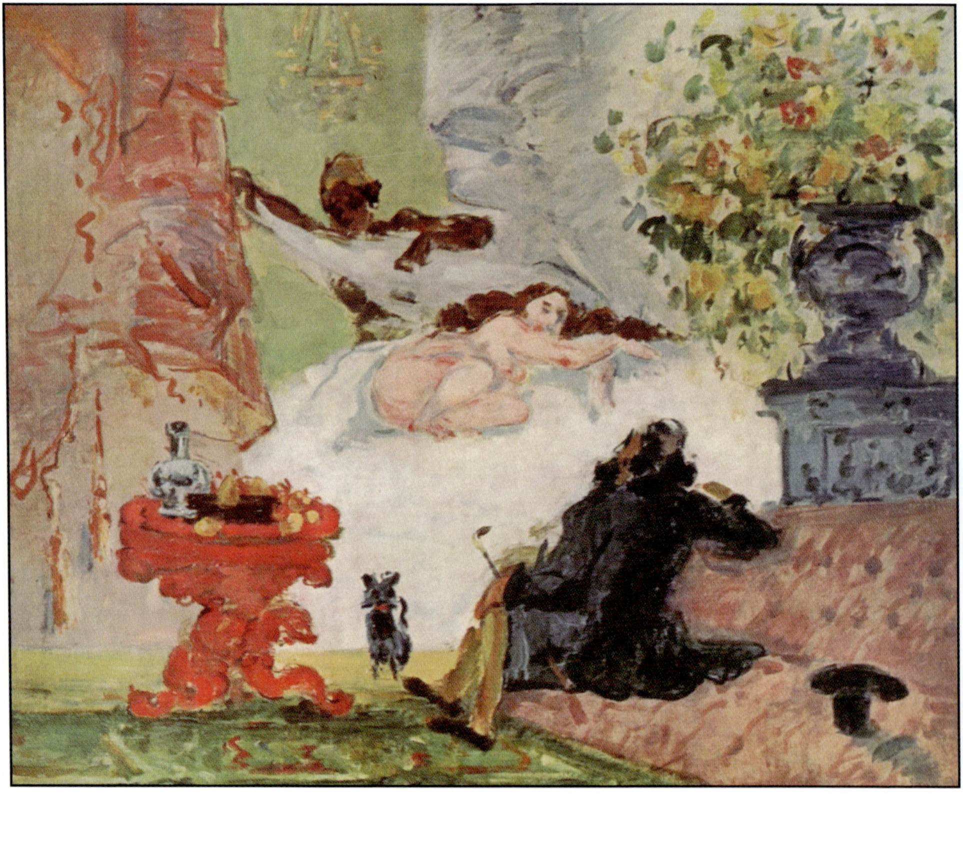

FLOWERS IN A BLUE VASE

1875, The State Hermitage Museum, St. Petersburg, Russia
55.2 x 46 cm

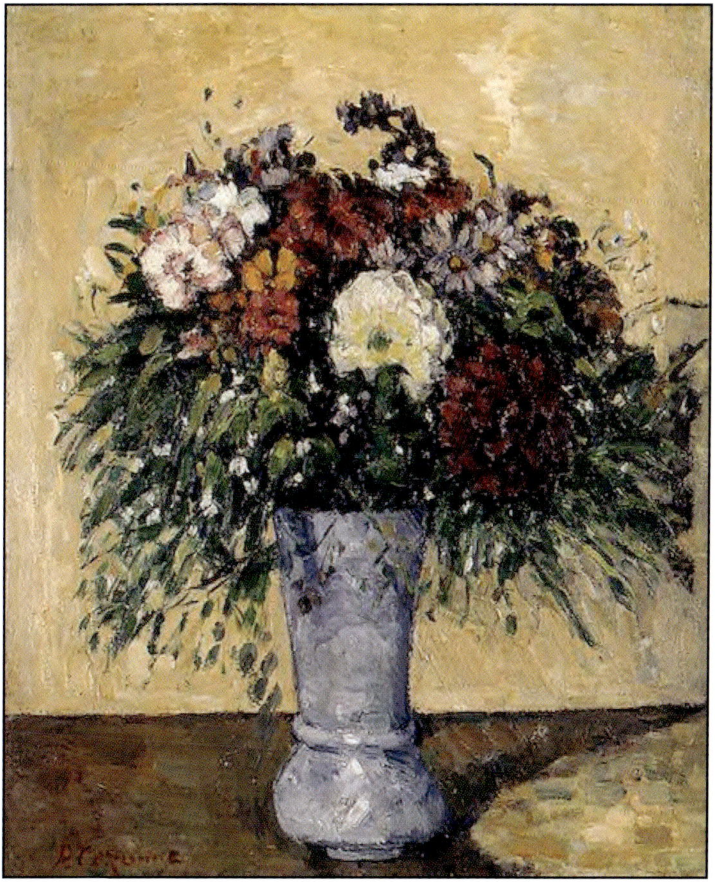

Plate 25

OLYMPIA

1875, Philadelphia Museum of Art
24.1 x 27 cm

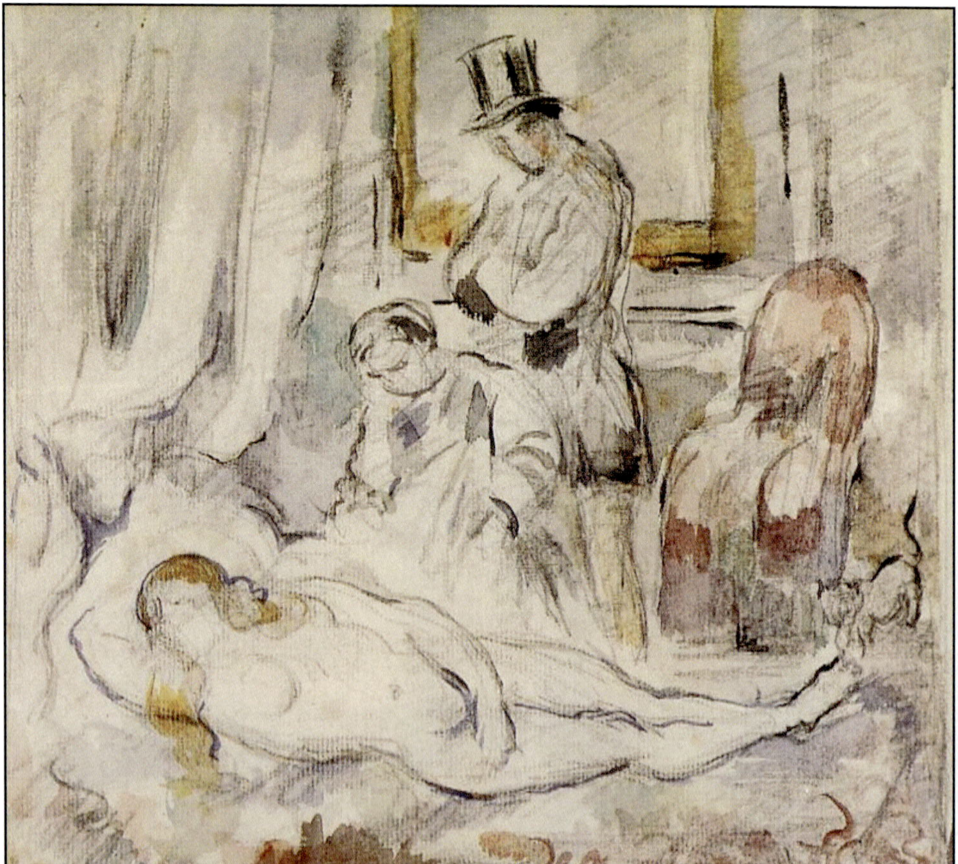

THE ETANG DES SOEURS AT OSNY

1875, Samuel Courtauld Trust, The Courtauld Gallery, London
60 x 73.5 cm

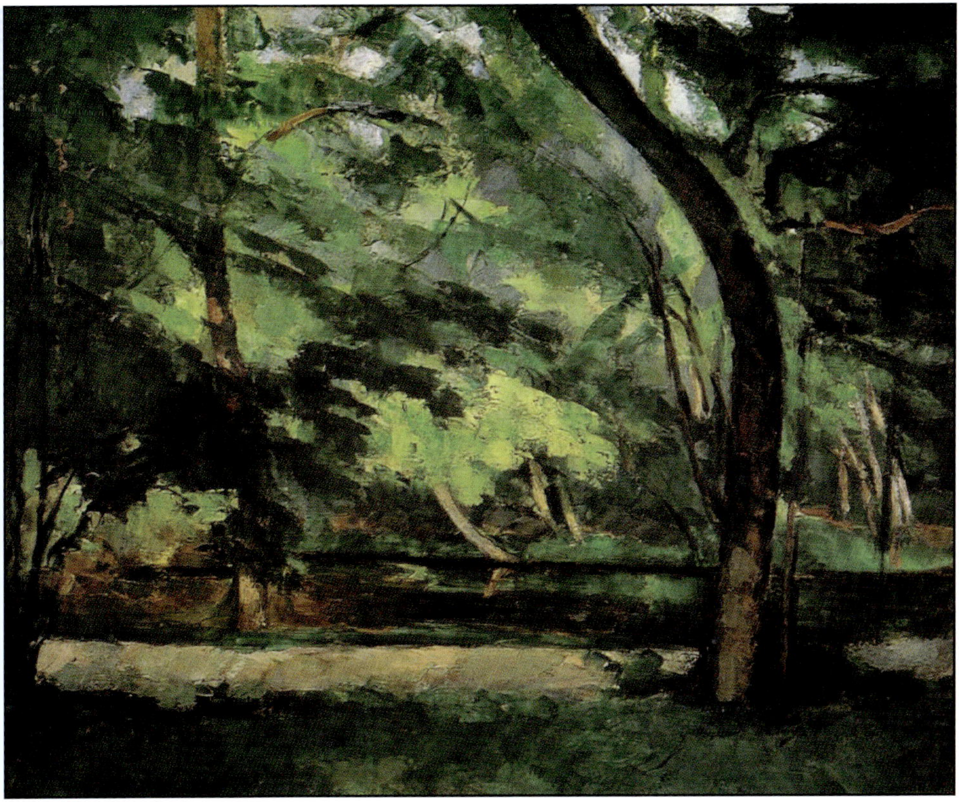

Plate 27

JAS DE BOUFFAN, THE POOL

1876, The State Hermitage Museum, St. Petersburg, Russia
46.1 x 56.3 cm

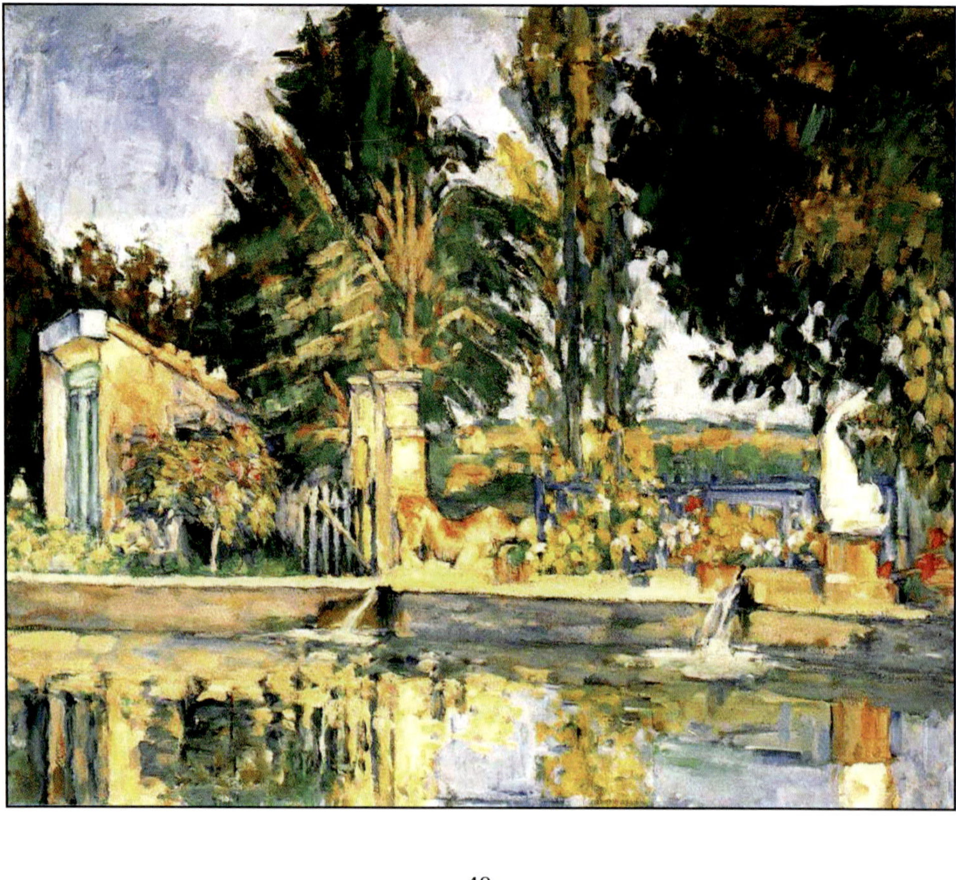

STILL LIFE

1877, Metropolitan Museum of Art, New York City
60.6 x 73.7 cm

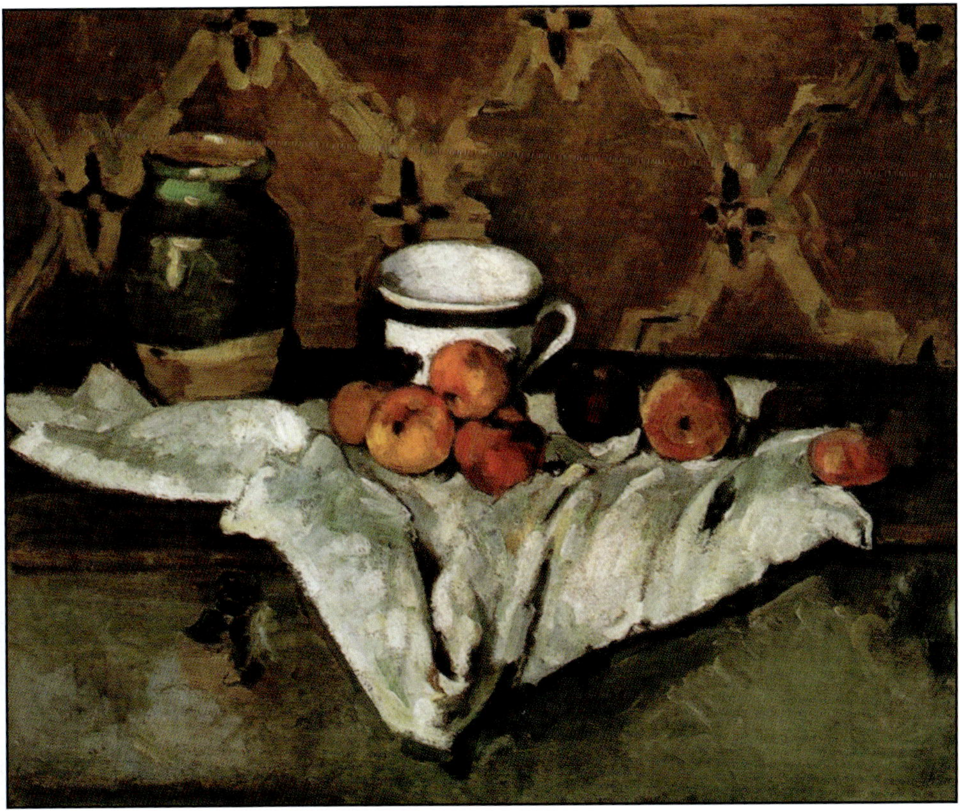

ORCHARD IN PONTOISE

1877, Private Collection
50 x 58 cm

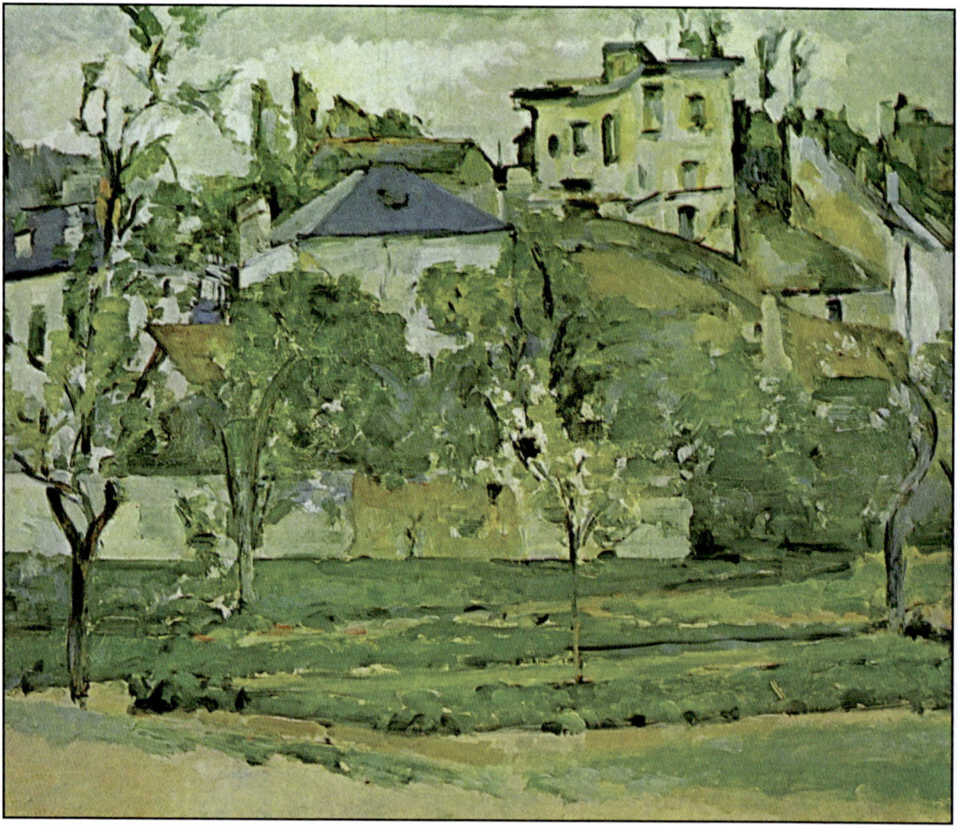

PORTRAIT OF MADAME CÉZANNE

1878, Museum of Fine Arts, Boston
72.5 x 56 cm

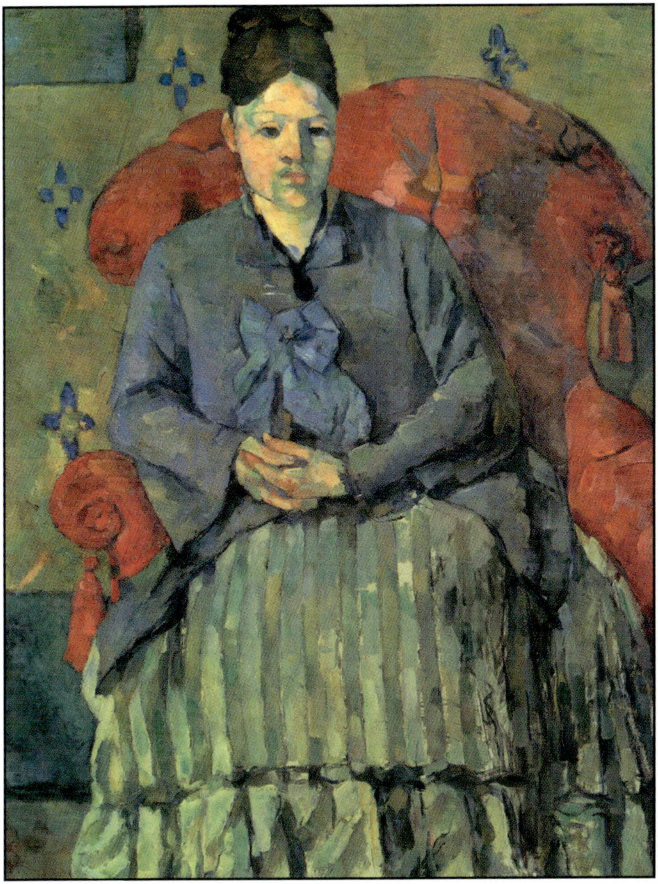

Plate 31

BOTTOM OF THE RAVINE

1879, Museum of Fine Arts, Houston
73 x 54 cm

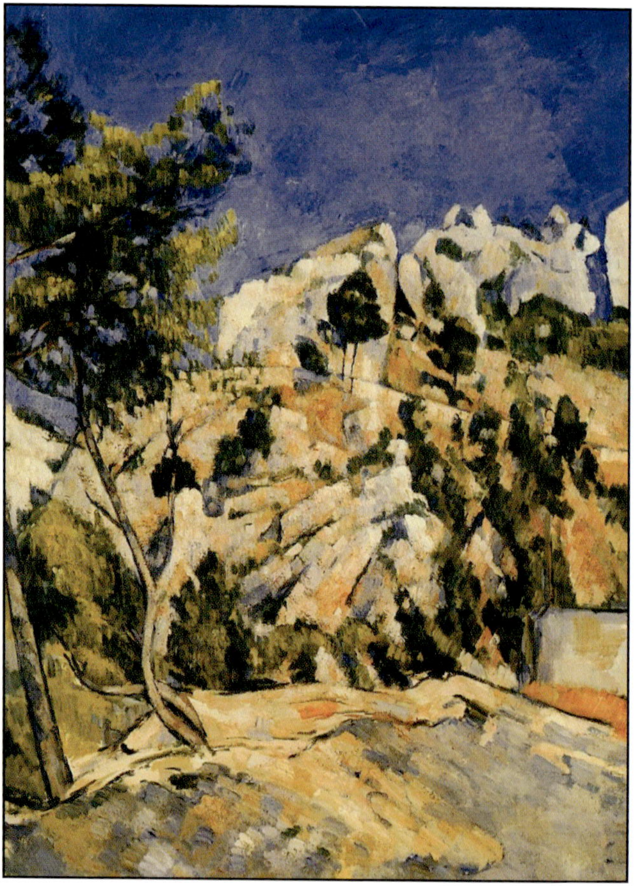

THE BRIDGE AT MAINCY

1879, Musée d'Orsay, Paris
58.5 x 72.5 cm

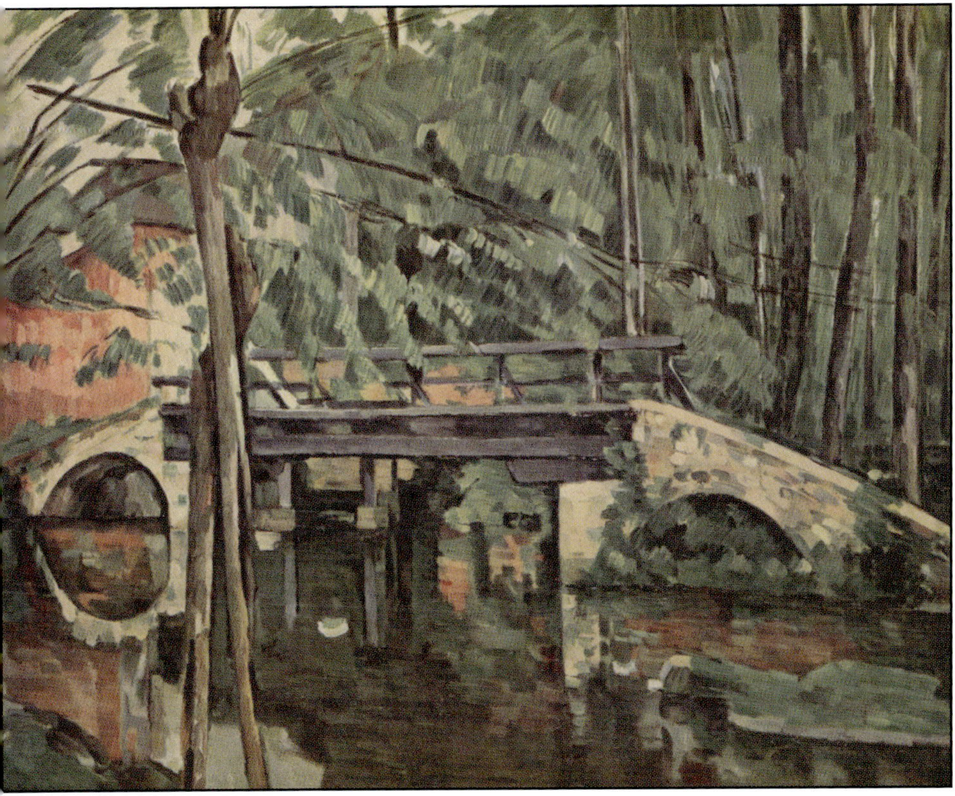

Plate 33

HOUSES IN PROVENCE

1880, National Gallery of Art, Washington, DC
65 x 81.3 cm

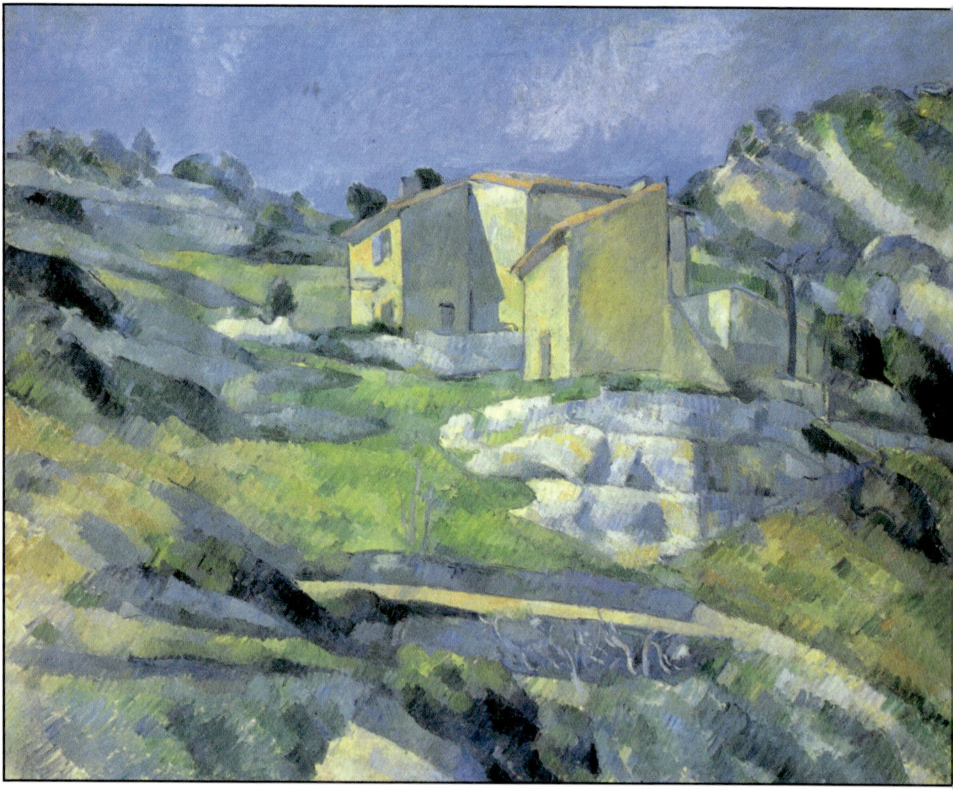

POPLARS

1880, Musée d'Orsay, Paris
62 x 78 cm

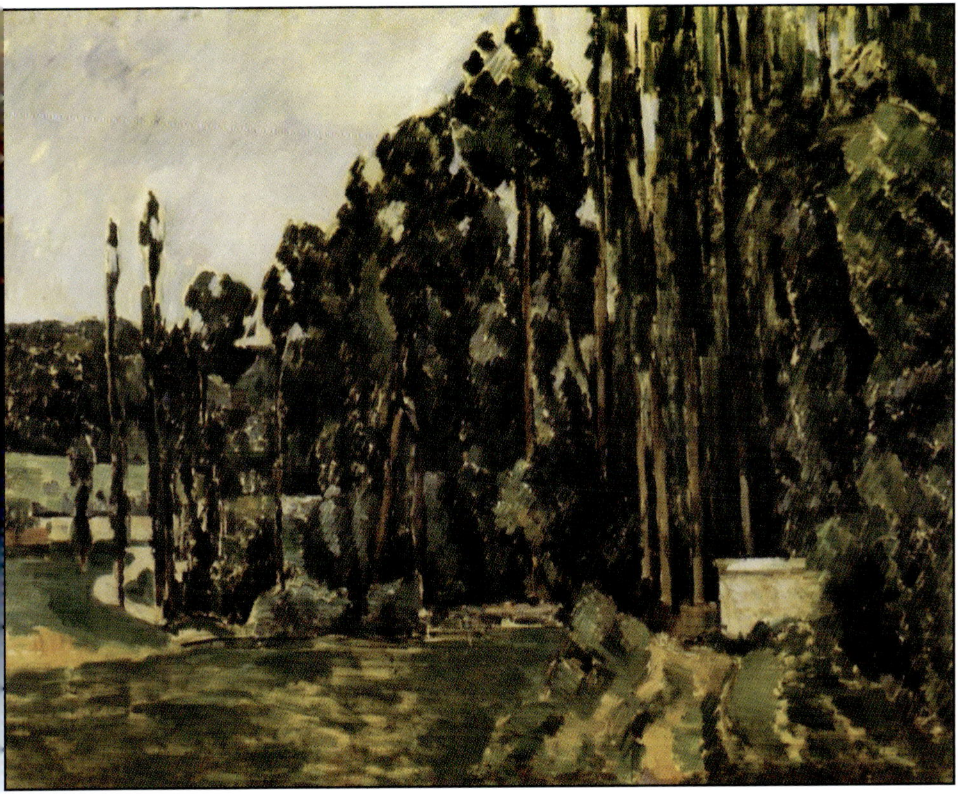

Plate 35

THE CHATEAU DE MÉDAN

1880, Burrell Collection, Glasgow, UK
59.1 x 72.4 cm

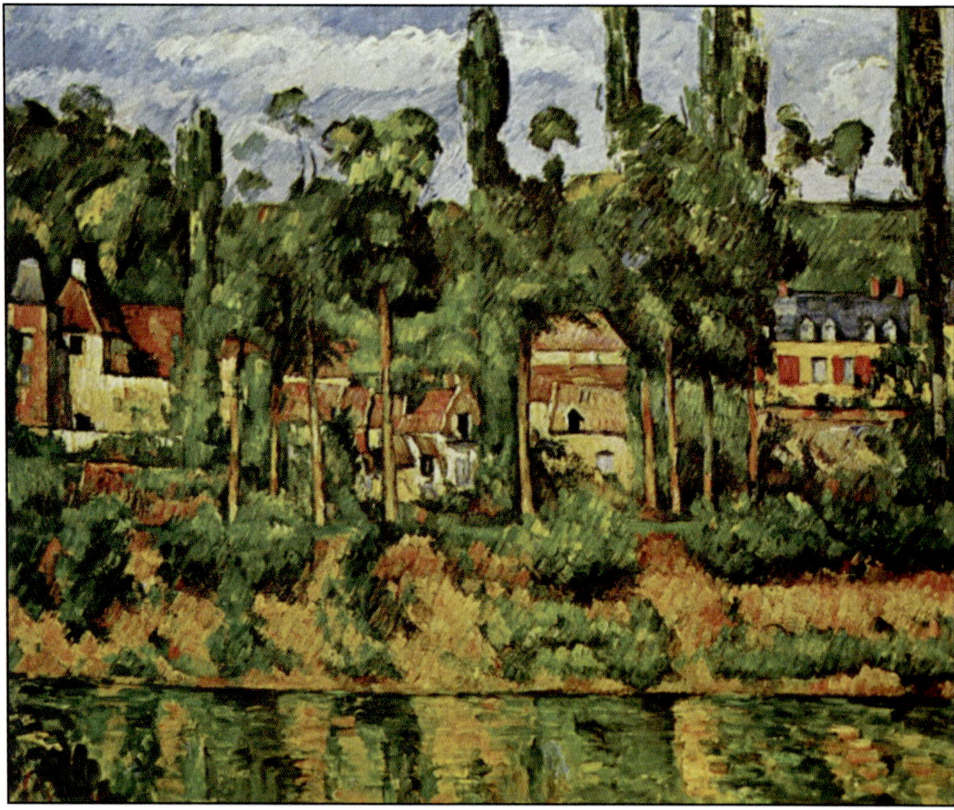

IN THE OISE VALLEY

1880, Metropolitan Museum of Art, New York City
32.4 x 50 cm

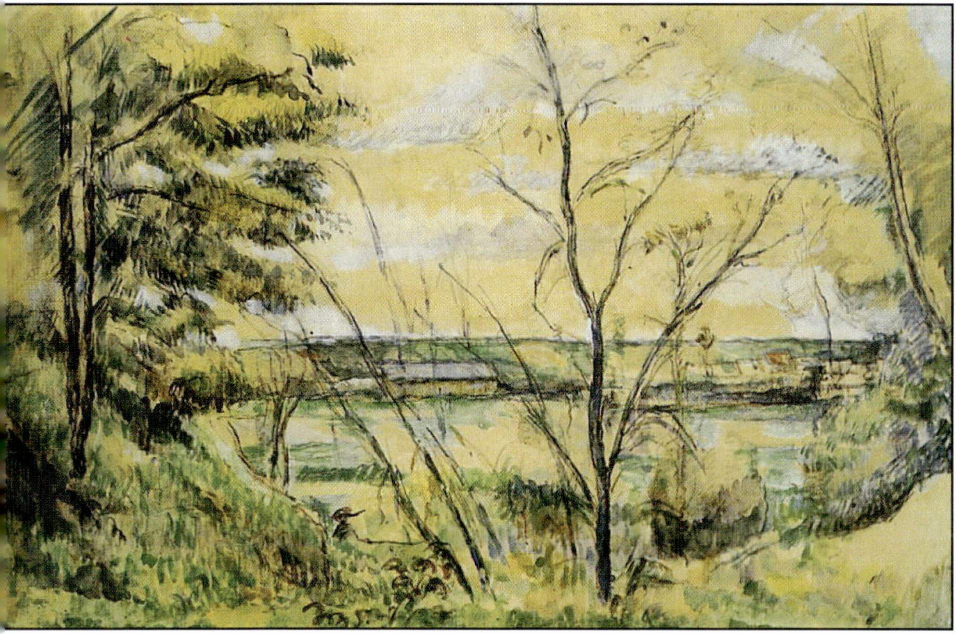

Plate 37

HOUSES ALONG A ROAD

1881, The State Hermitage Museum, St. Petersburg, Russia
60 x 73.5 cm

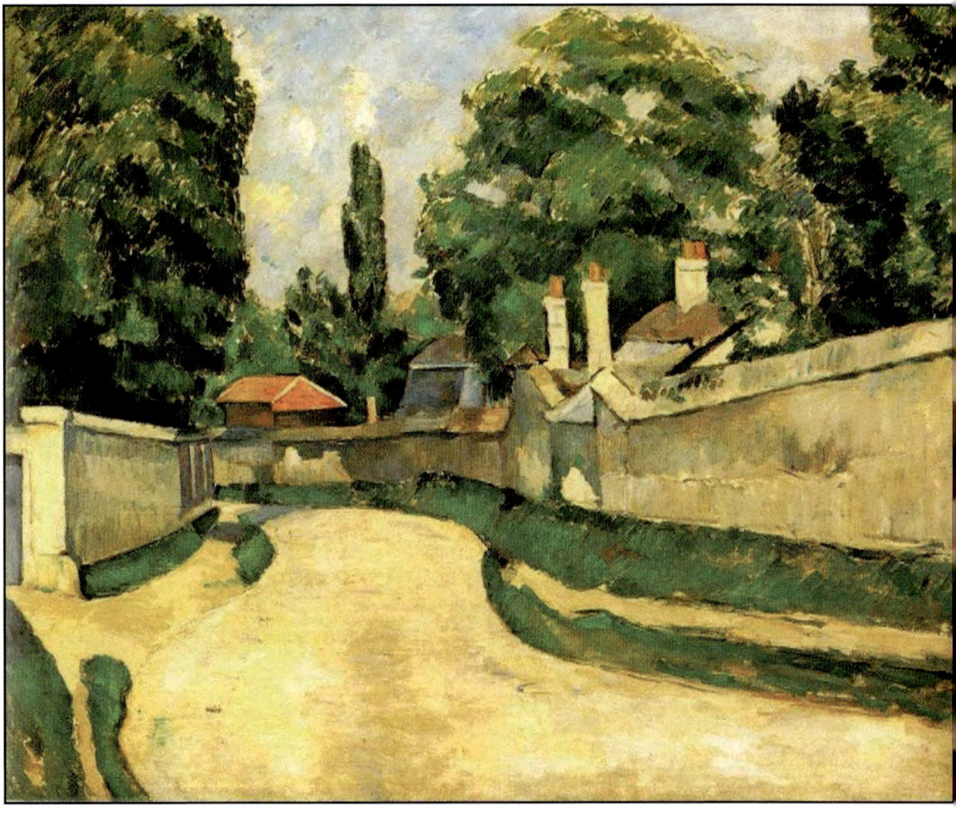

LANDSCAPE

1882, Nationalmuseum, Stockholm
73 x 92 cm

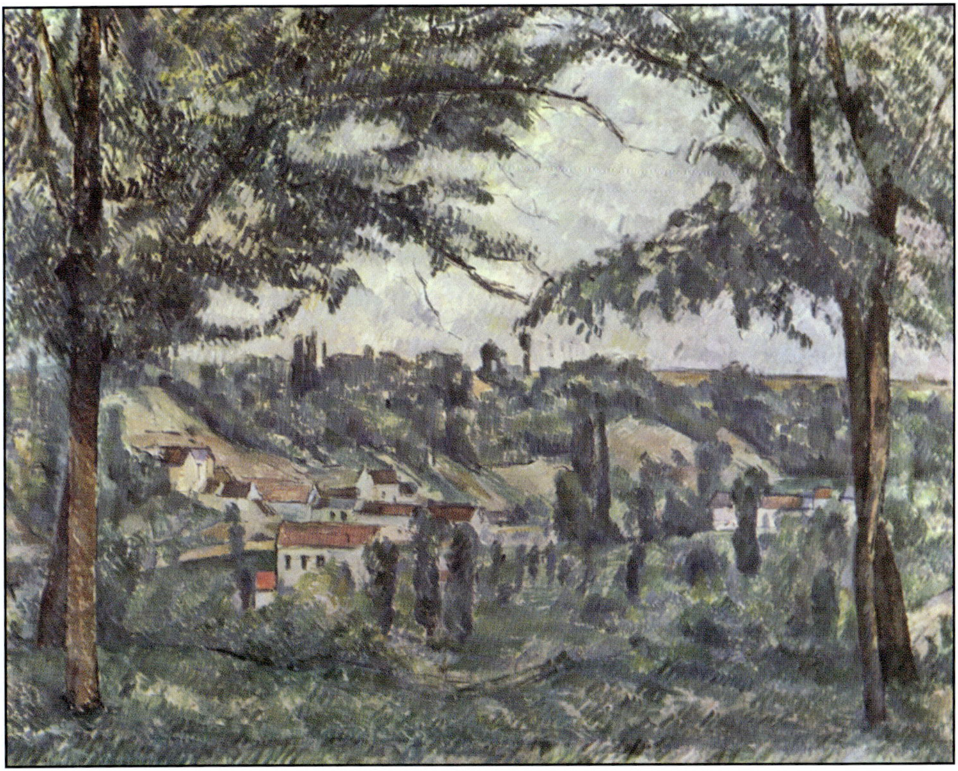

LEDA AND THE SWAN

1882, The Barnes Foundation, Philadelphia
59.7 x 74.9 cm

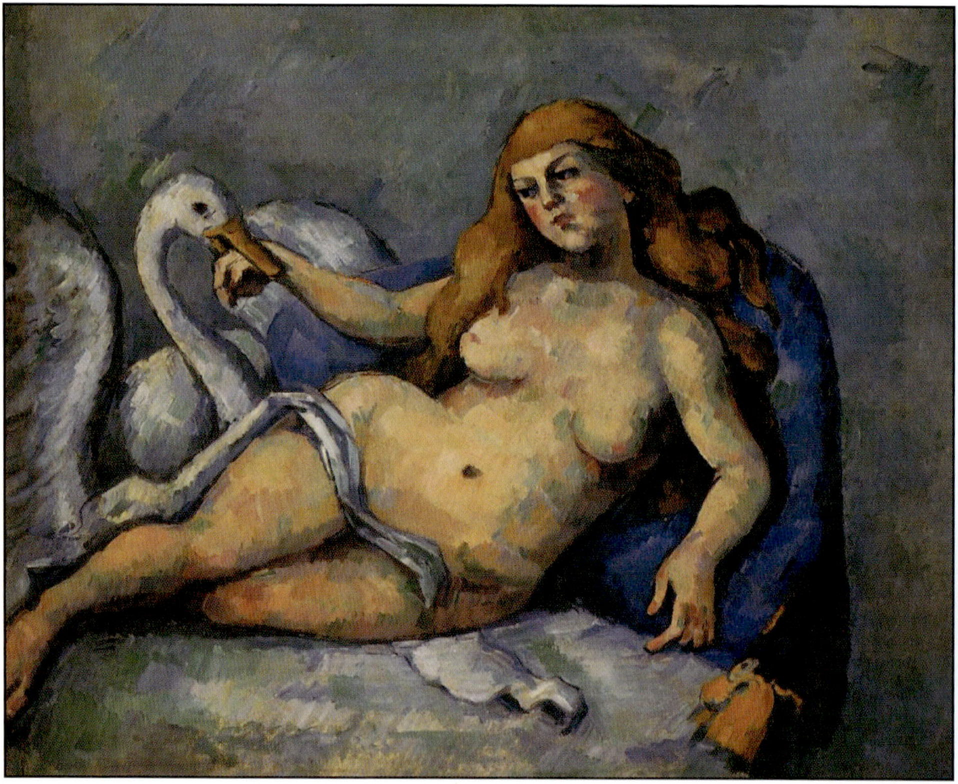

THE GULF OF MARSEILLE SEEN FROM L'ESTAQUE

1885, Metropolitan Museum of Art, New York City
73 x 100.3 cm

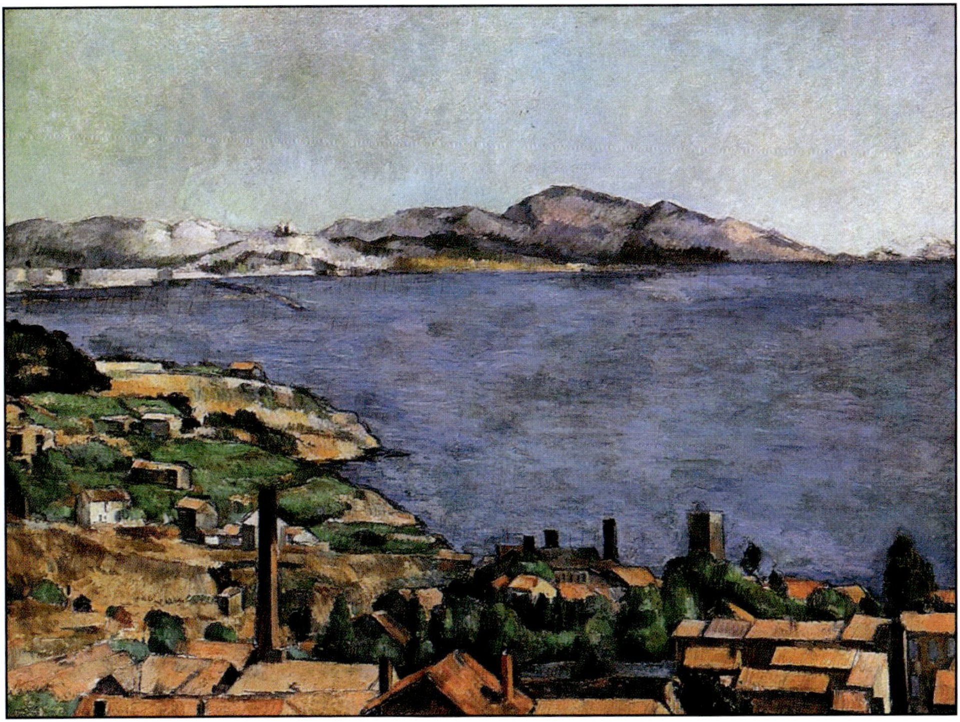

GARDANNE

1886, Metropolitan Museum of Art, New York City
80 x 64.2 cm

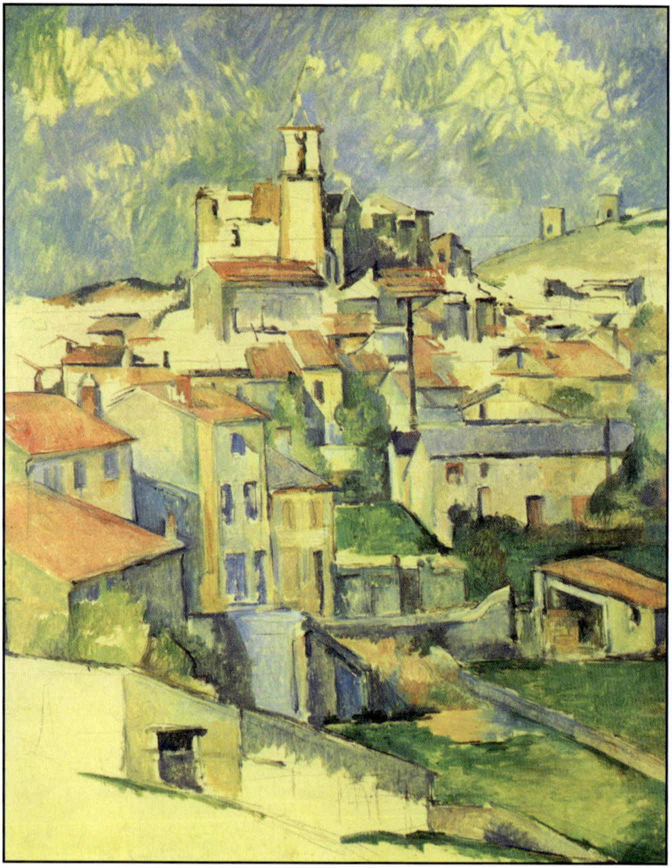

CHESTNUT TREES AT THE JAS DE BOUFFAN

1887, Minneapolis Institute of the Arts
73 x 92 cm

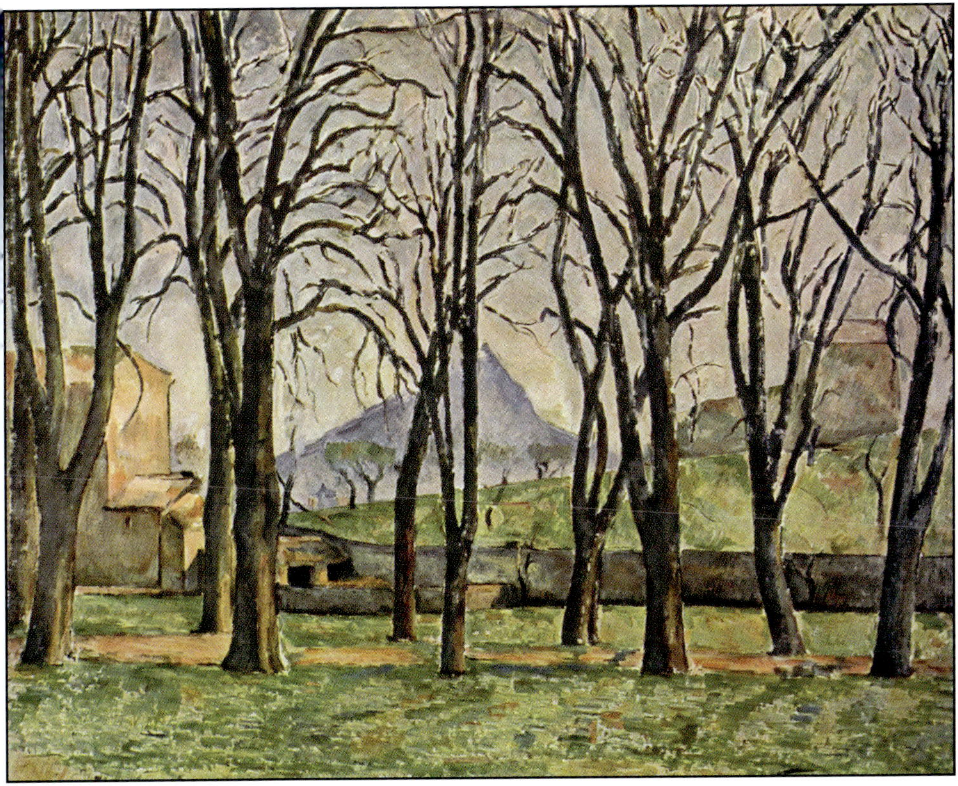

Plate 43

LANDSCAPE WITH VIADUCT: MONTAGNE SAINTE-VICTOIRE

1887, Metropolitan Museum of Art, New York City
65 x 82 cm

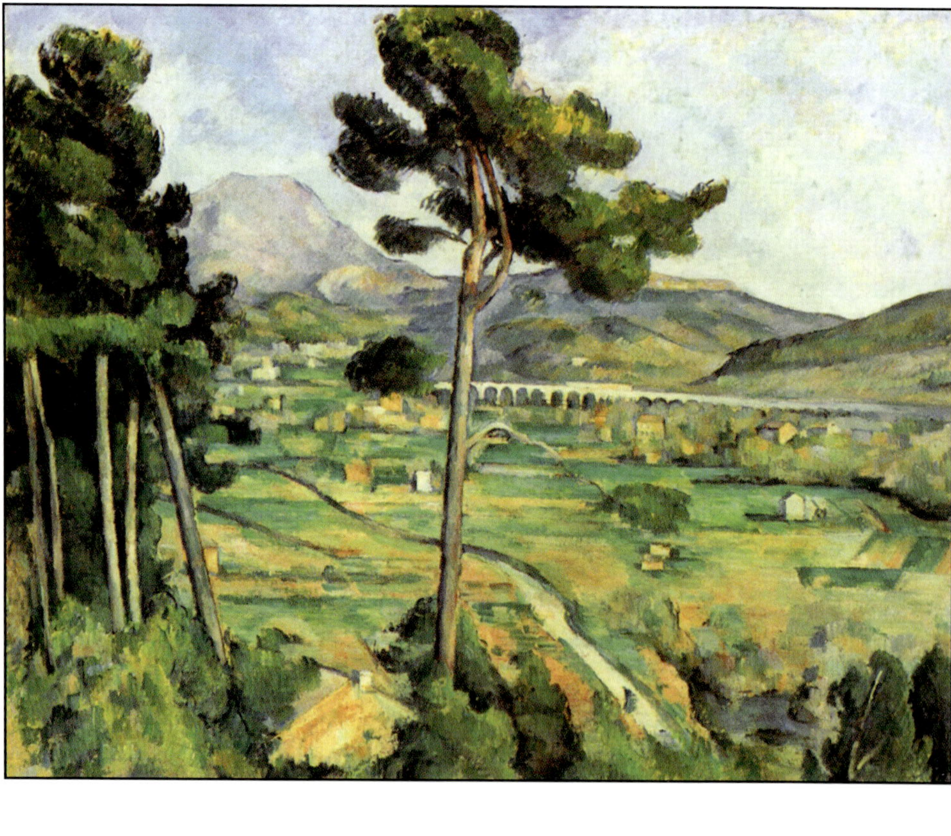

PIERROT AND HARLEQUIN (MARDI GRAS)

1888, Pushkin Museum of Fine Arts, Moscow
102 x 81 cm

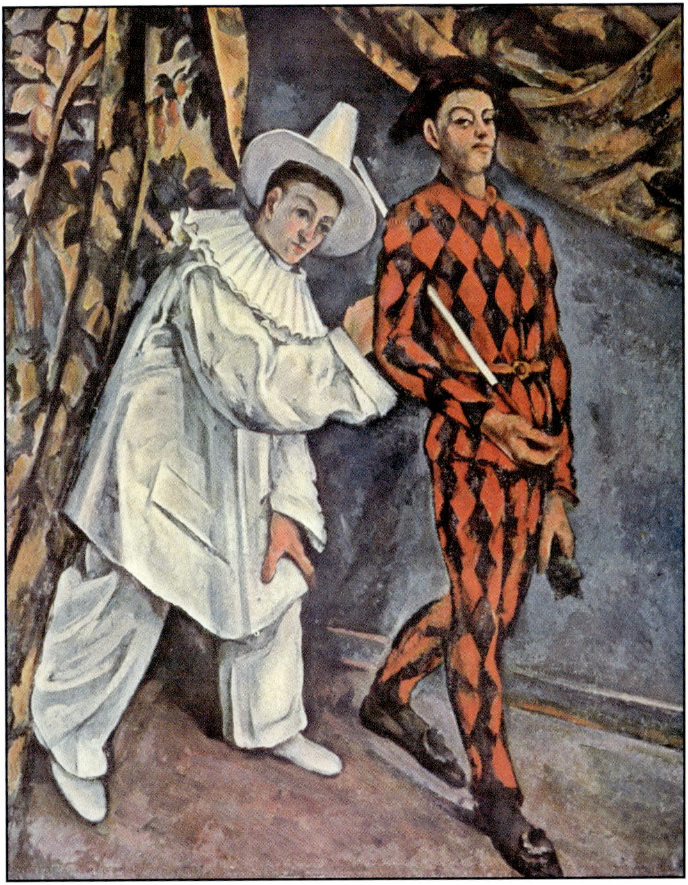

Plate 45

POTS OF GERANIUMS

1888, National Gallery of Art, Washington, DC
30.5 x 28.5 cm

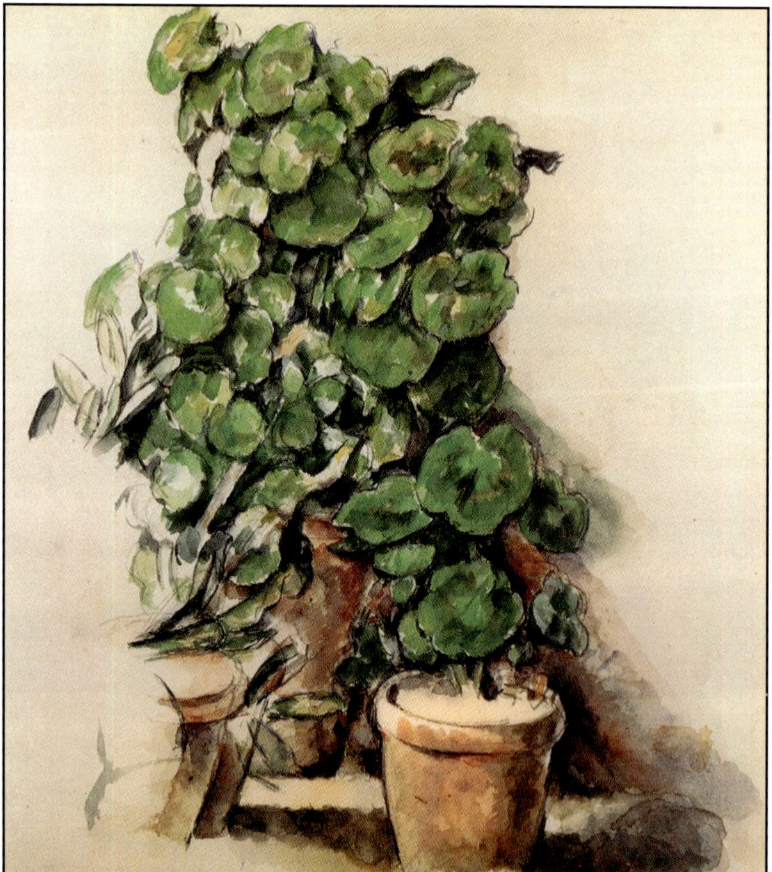

THE ALLEY AT CHANTILLY

1888, Toledo Museum of Art, Ohio
81 x 65 cm

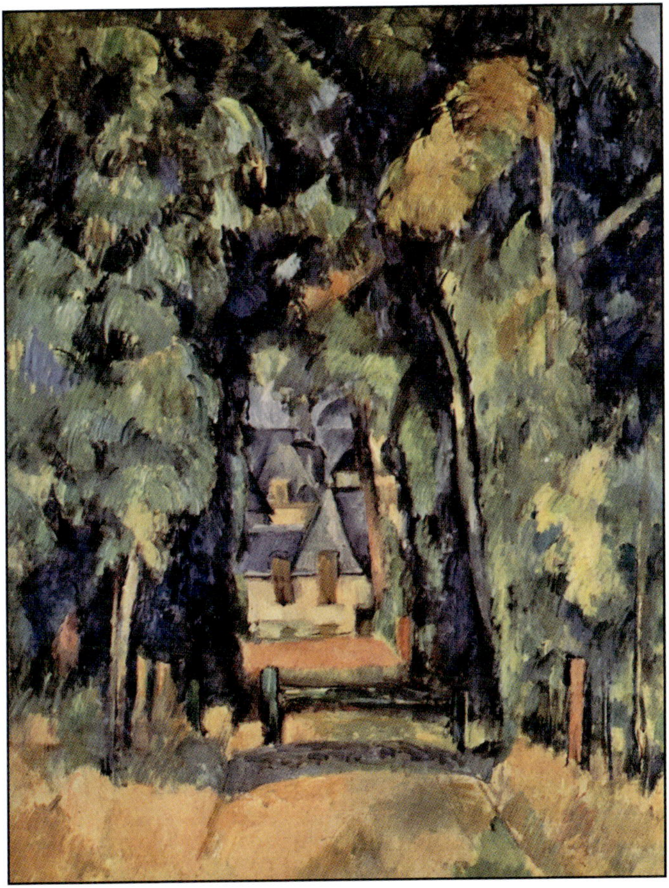

BOY IN A RED VEST

1889, Private Collection
80 x 64.5 cm

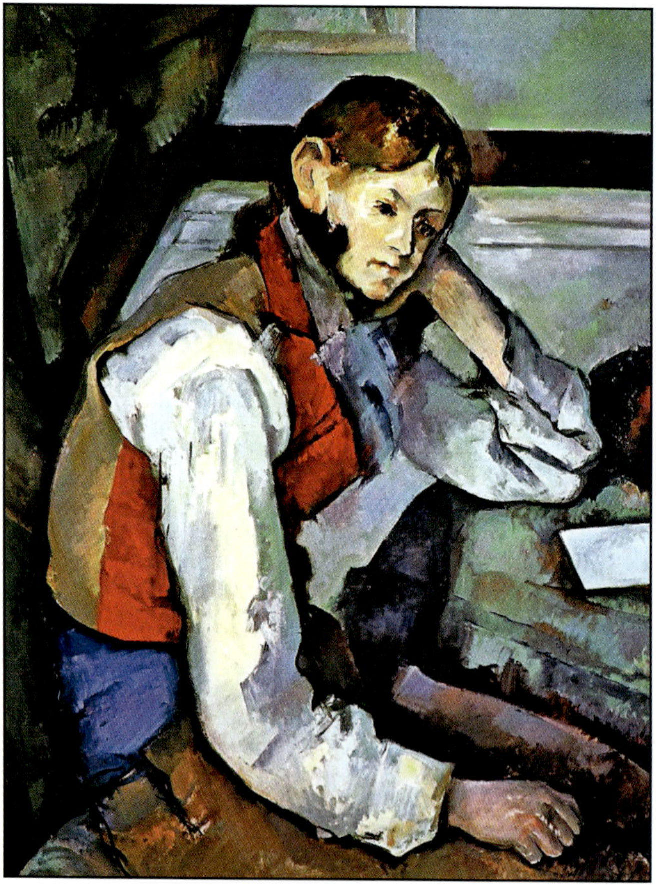

HILLSIDE IN PROVENCE

1890, National Gallery, London
65 x 81 cm

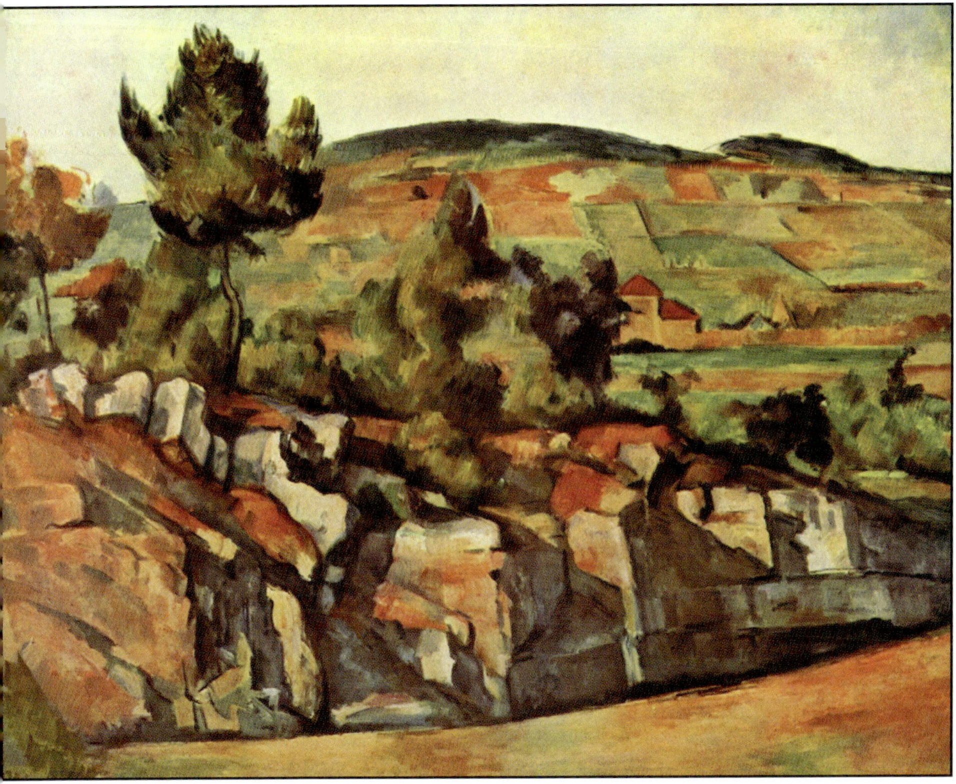

Plate 49

STILL LIFE WITH BASKET

1890, Musée d'Orsay, Paris
65 x 81 cm

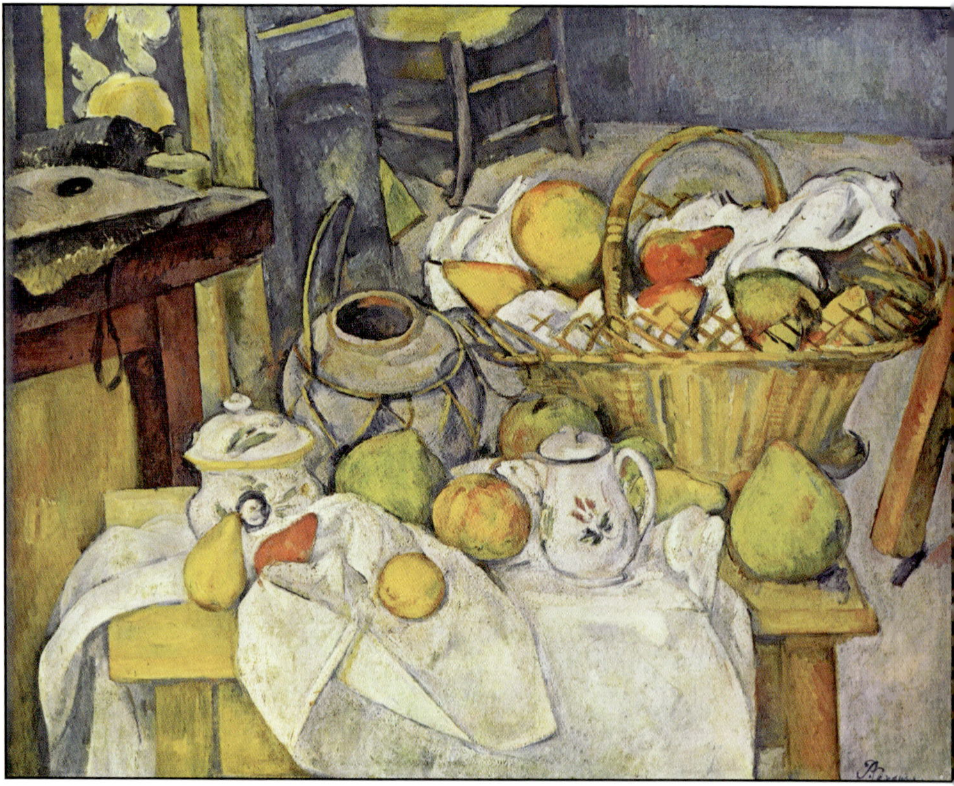

THE PIGEON TOWER AT BELLEVUE

1890, Cleveland Museum of Art. Ohio
64 x 80 cm

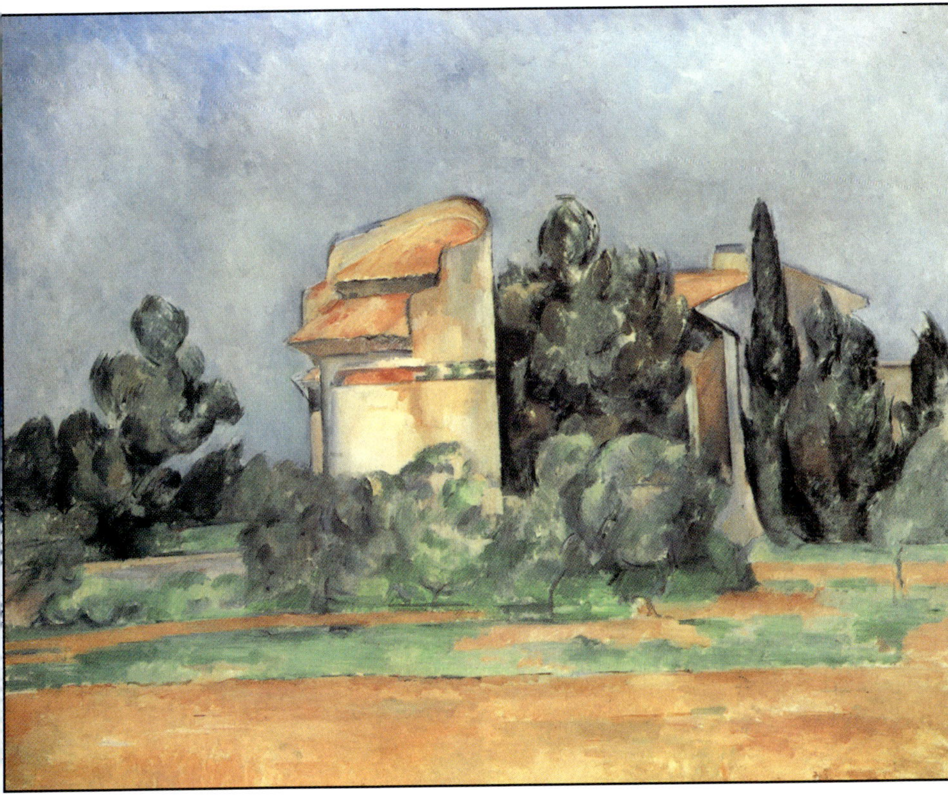

THE SMOKER

1890, The State Hermitage Museum, St. Petersburg, Russia
90 x 72 cm

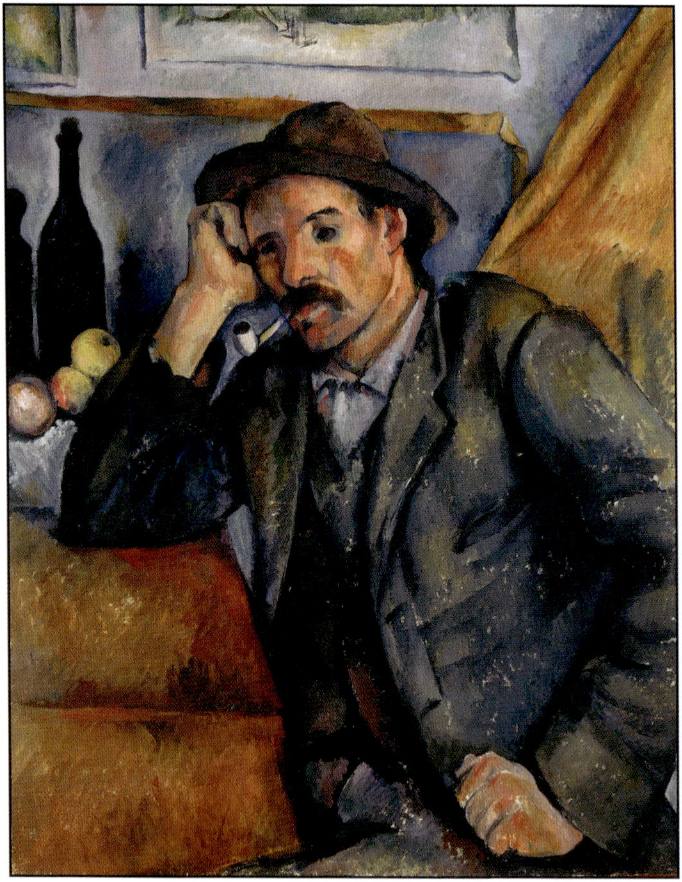

THE CARD PLAYERS

1892, The Barnes Foundation, Philadelphia
135.3 x 181.9 cm

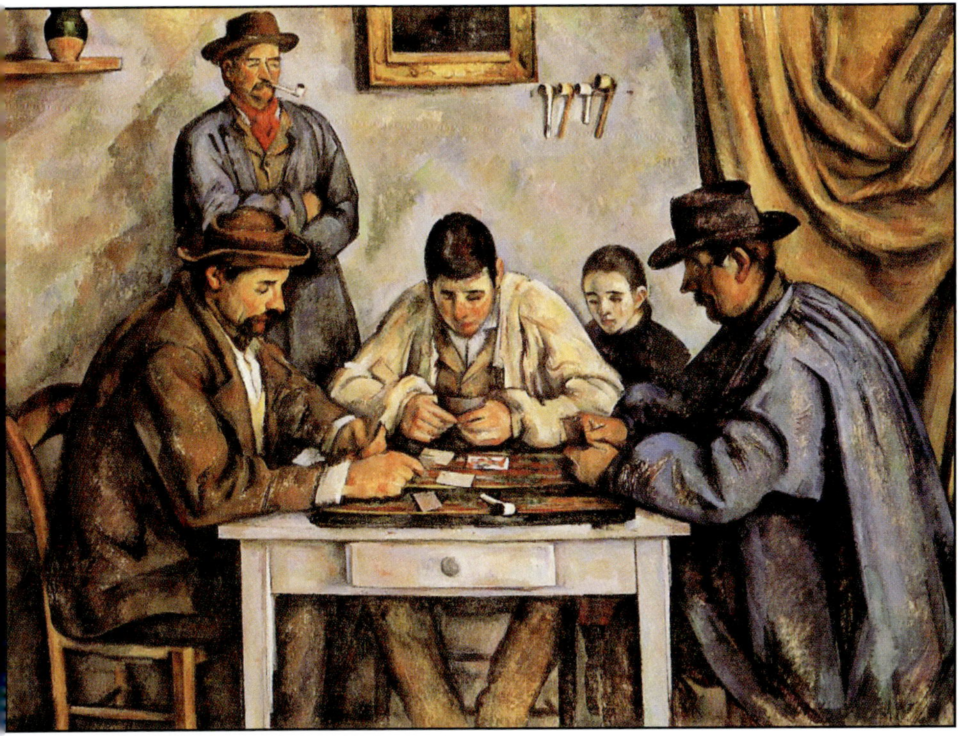

ROCKS AT FOUNTAINEBLEAU

1893, Metropolitan Museum of Art, New York City
73 x 91 cm

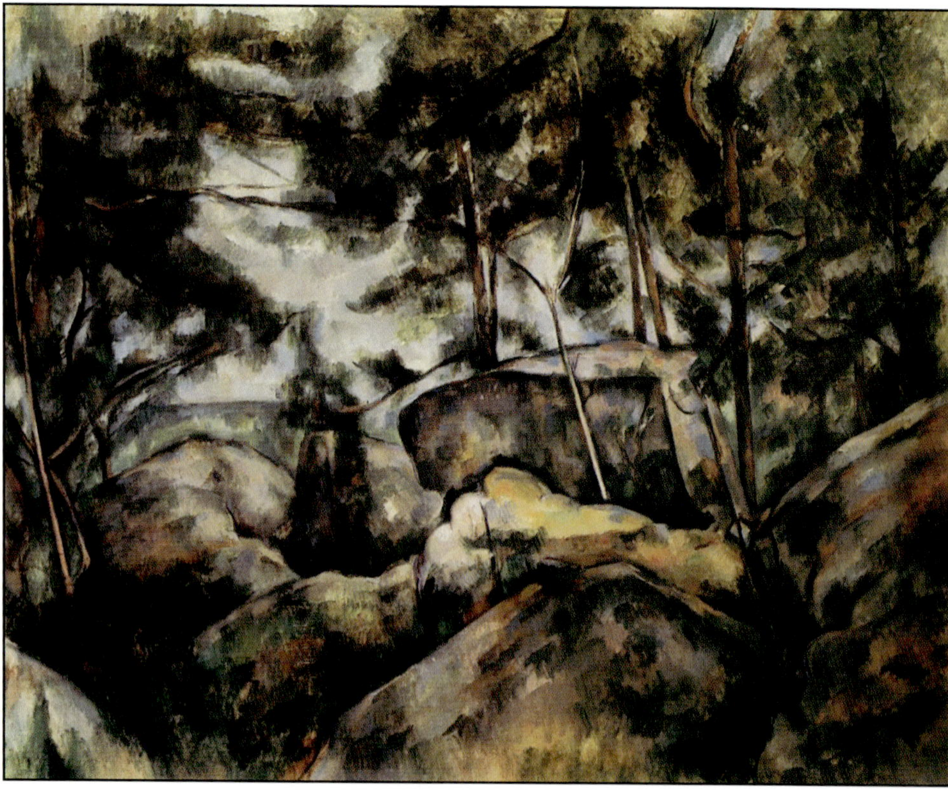

MILLSTONE AND CISTERN UNDER TREES

1894, The Barnes Foundation, Philadelphia
65.1 x 81 cm

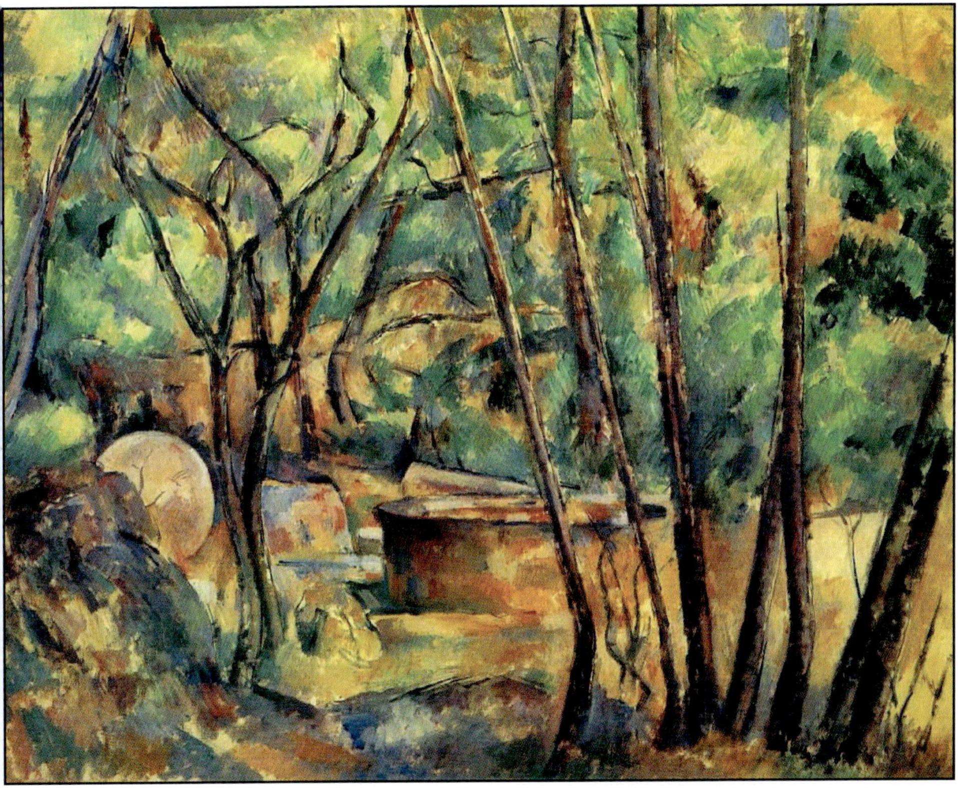

THE HOUSE WITH CRACKED WALLS

1894, Philadelphia Museum of Art
65 x 54 cm

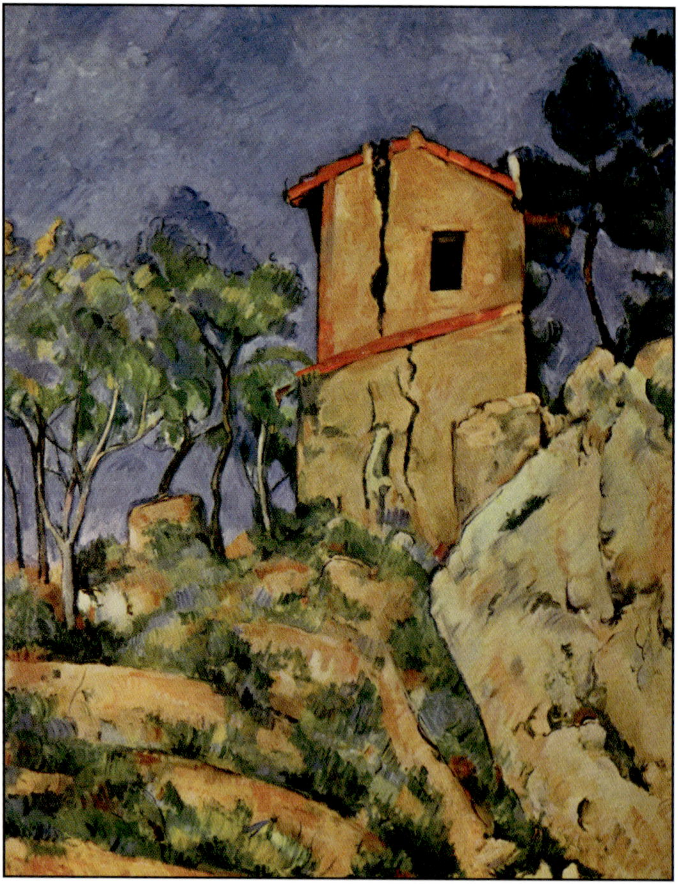

STILL LIFE: APPLES AND A POT OF PRIMROSES

1894, Private Collection
58.5 x 42 cm

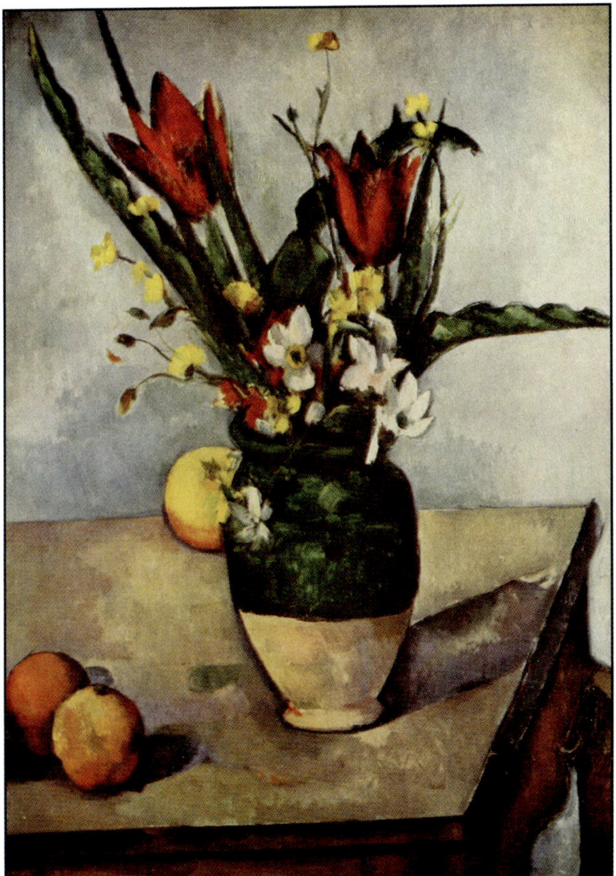

Plate 57

WOMAN IN A GREEN HAT (MADAME CÉZANNE)

1895, The Barnes Foundation, Philadelphia
100.3 x 81.3 cm

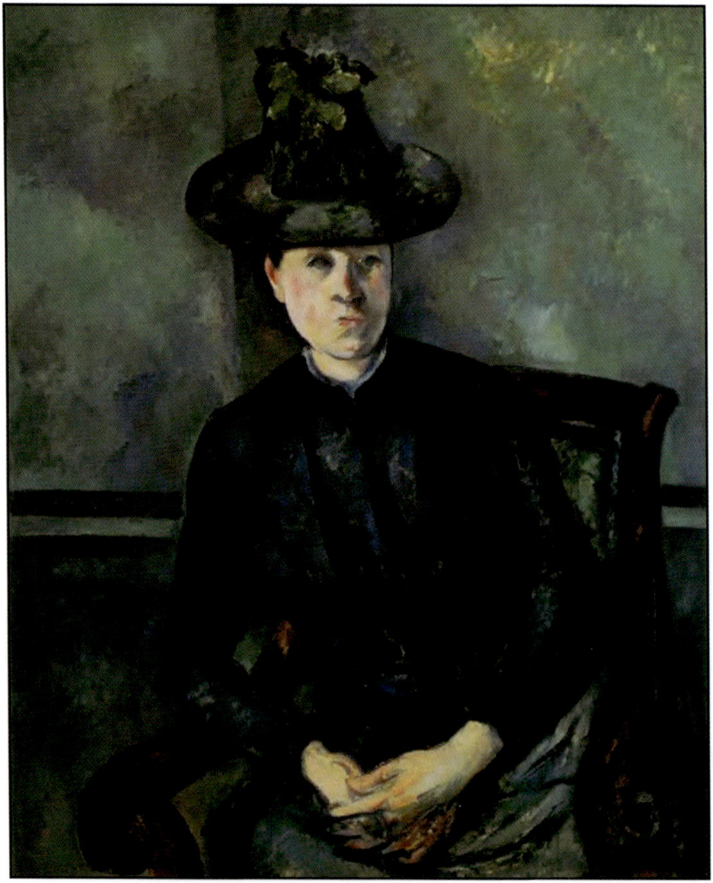

MAISON MARIA WITH A VIEW OF CHATEAU NOIR

1895, Kimbell Art Museum, Fort Worth, Texas
65 x 81 cm

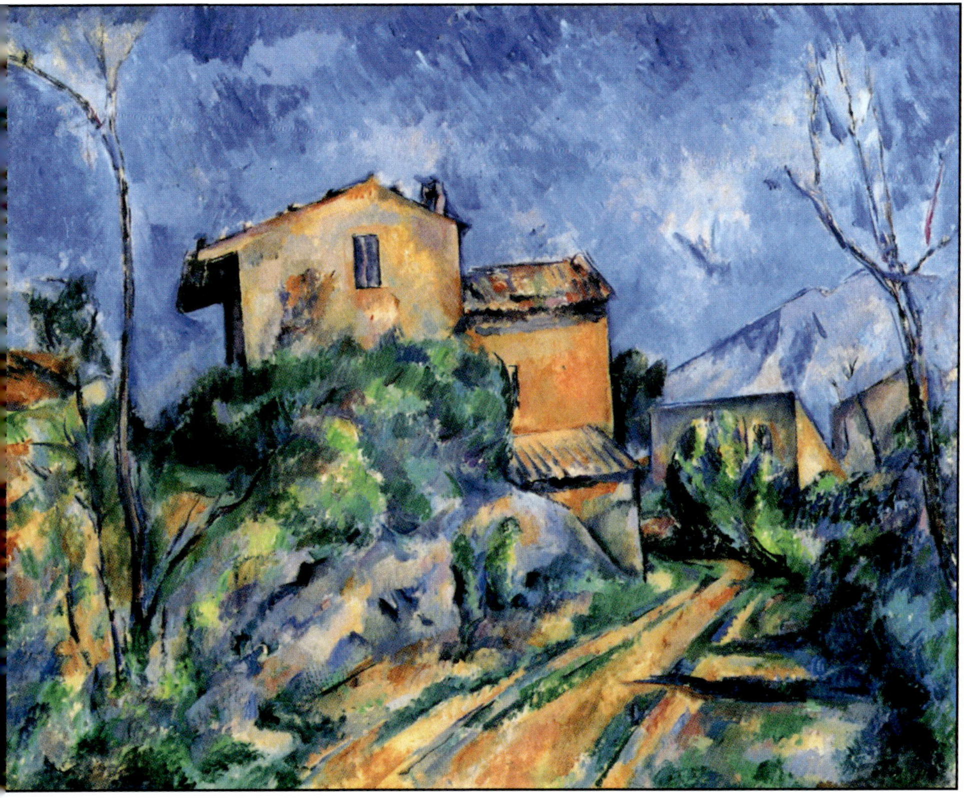

MONT SAINTE-VICTOIRE

1895, The Barnes Foundation, Philadelphia
73 x 92 cm

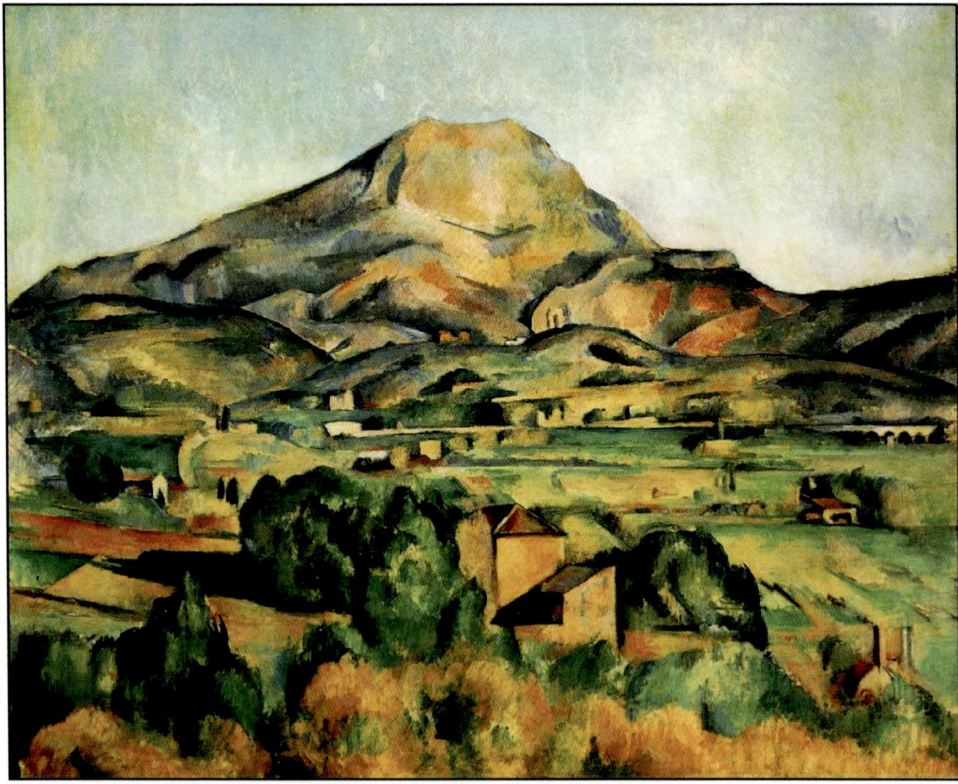

PORTRAIT OF GUSTAVE GEFFROY

1895, Musée d'Orsay, Paris
116 x 82 cm

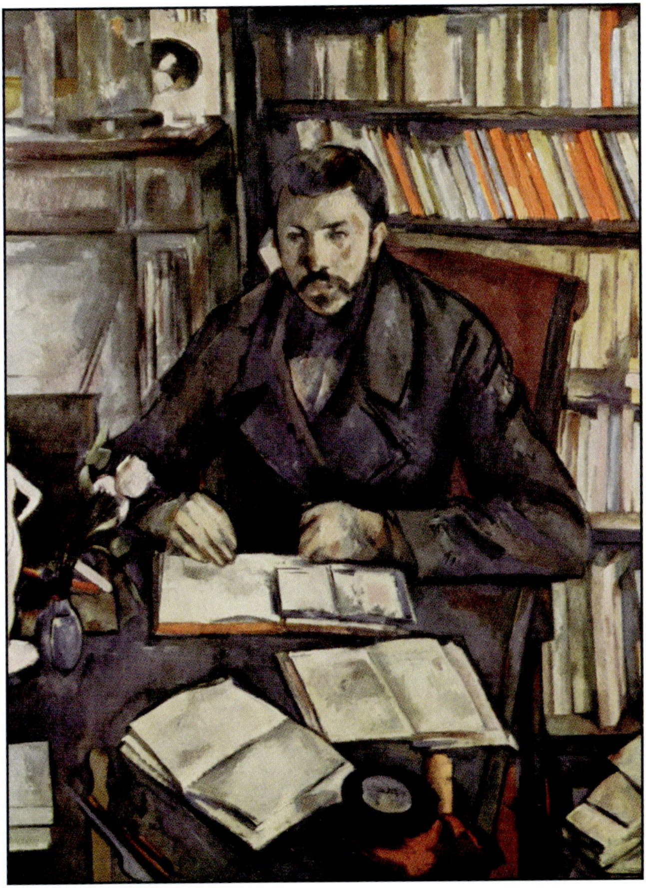

Plate 61

STILL LIFE WITH A BASKET OF APPLES

1895, Art Institute of Chicago
65 cm x 80 cm

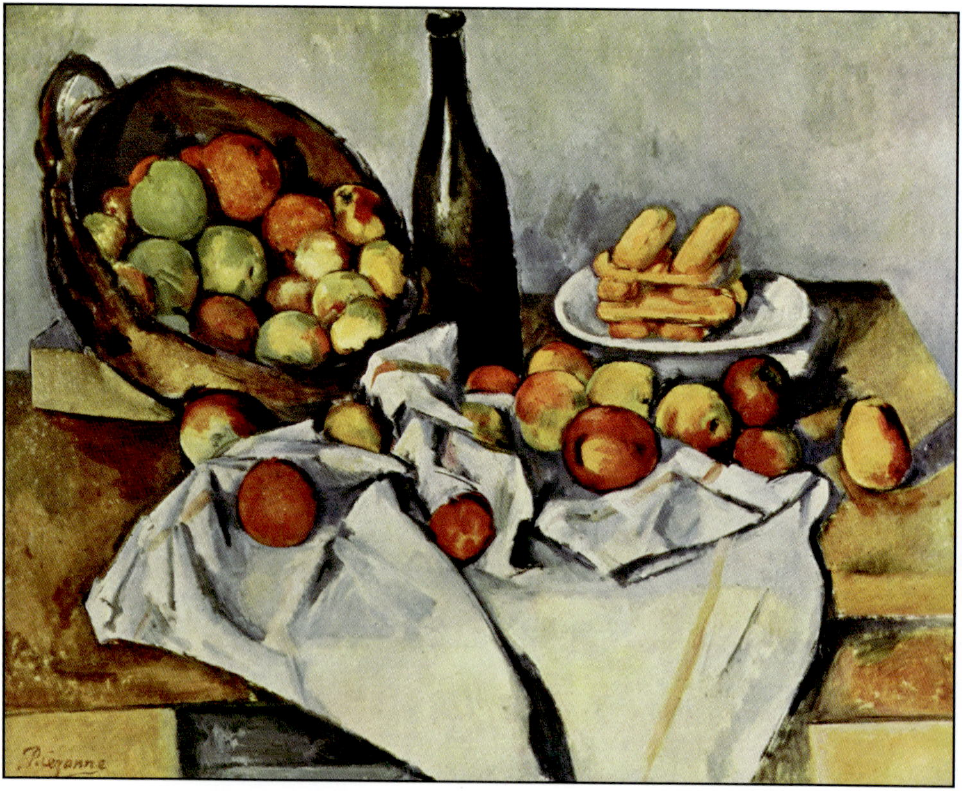

FOLIAGE

1895, Museum of Modern Art, New York City
44.8 x 56.8 cm

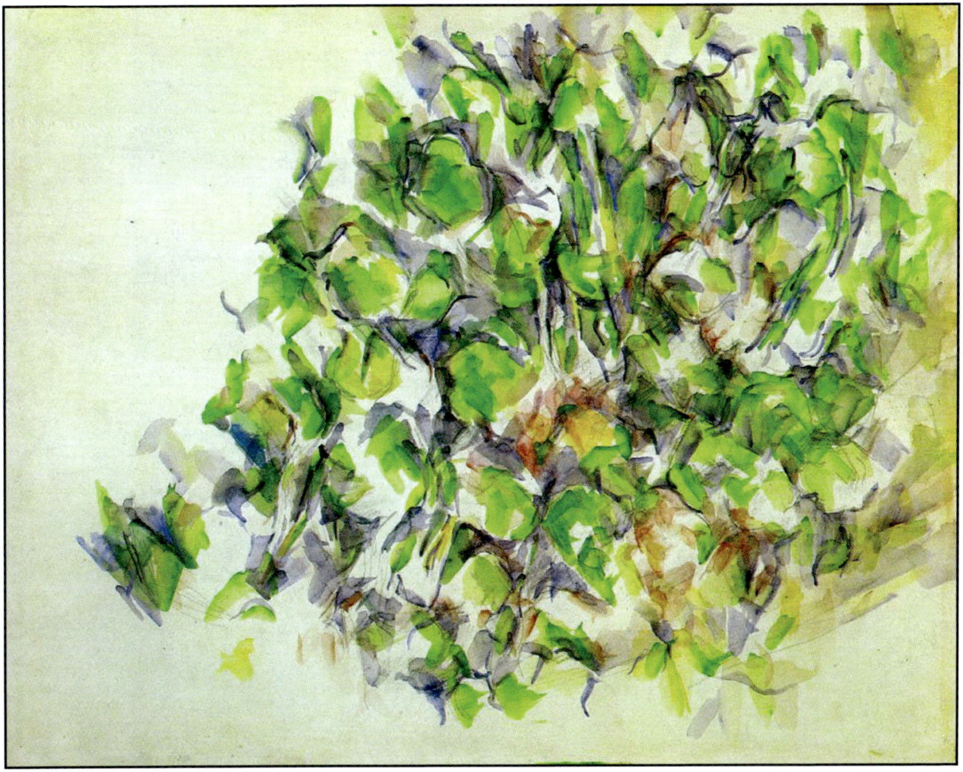

Plate 63

OLD WOMAN WITH A ROSARY

1896, National Gallery, London
80.6 x 65.5 cm

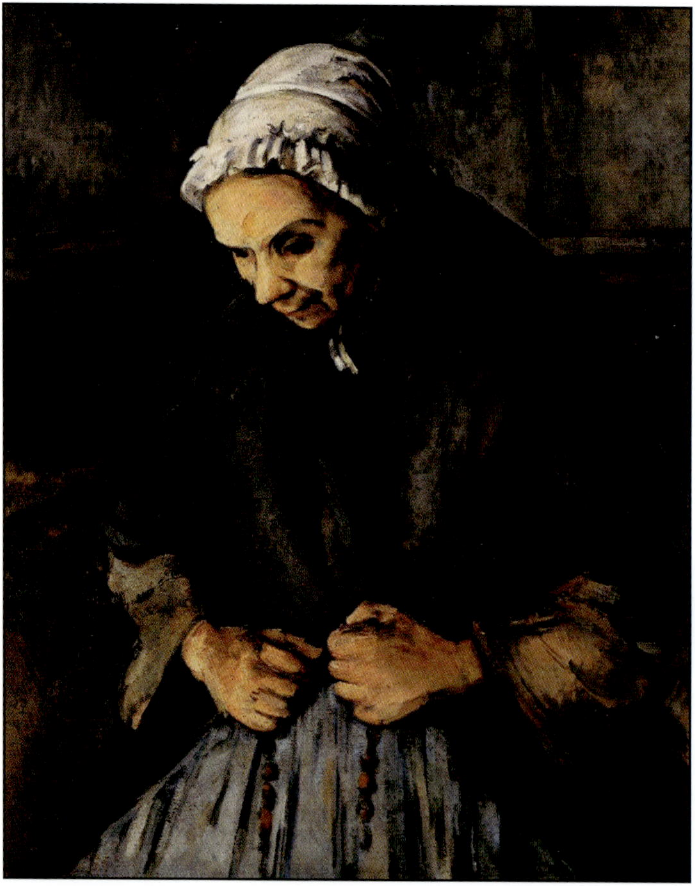

PEASANT IN A BLUE SMOCK

1897, Kimbell Art Museum, Fort Worth, Texas
81 x 65 cm

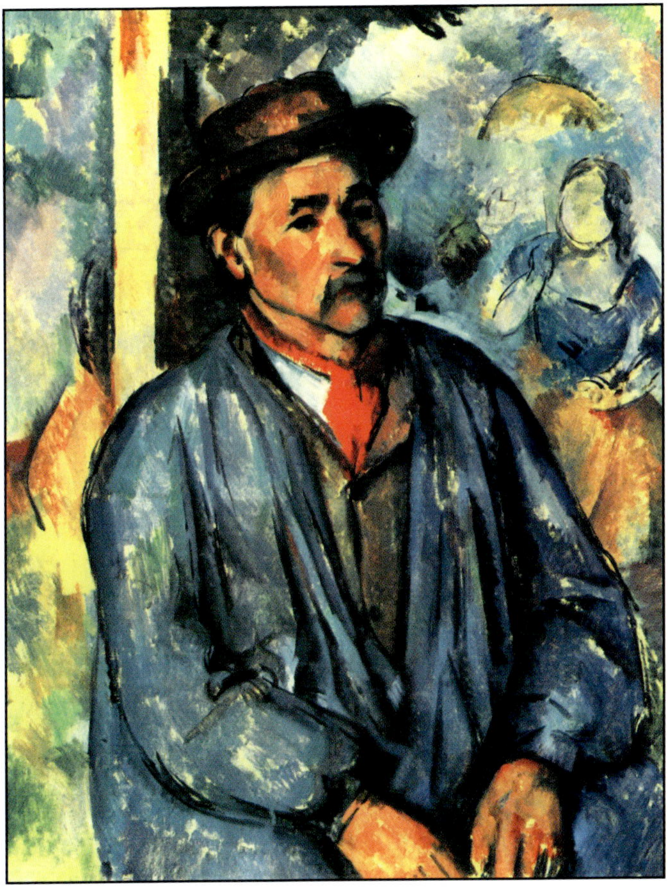

LARGE BATHERS

1900, National Gallery, London
136 x 191 cm

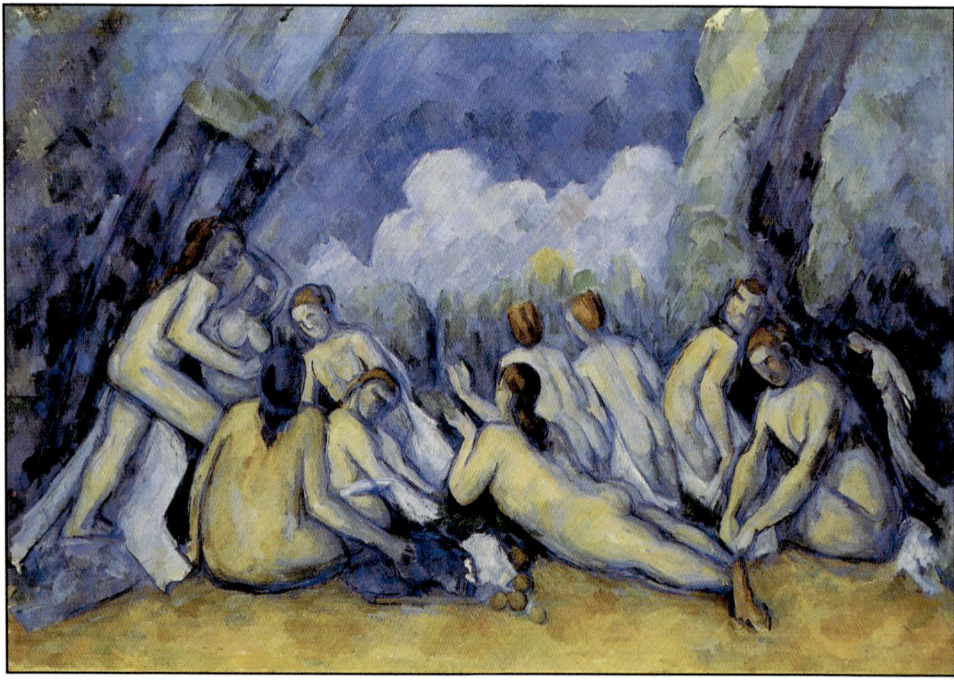

PYRAMID OF SKULLS

1900, Grand Palais, Paris
39 x 46.5 cm

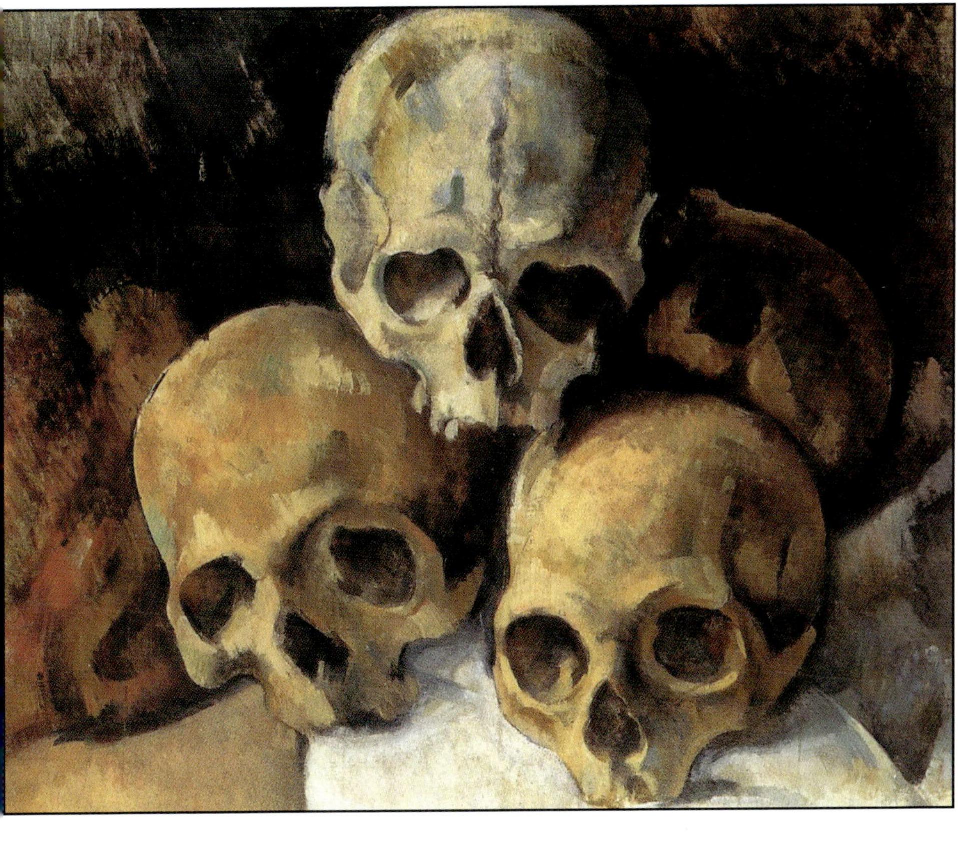

Plate 67

SEATED PEASANT

1900, Philadelphia Museum of Art
54.6 x 45 cm

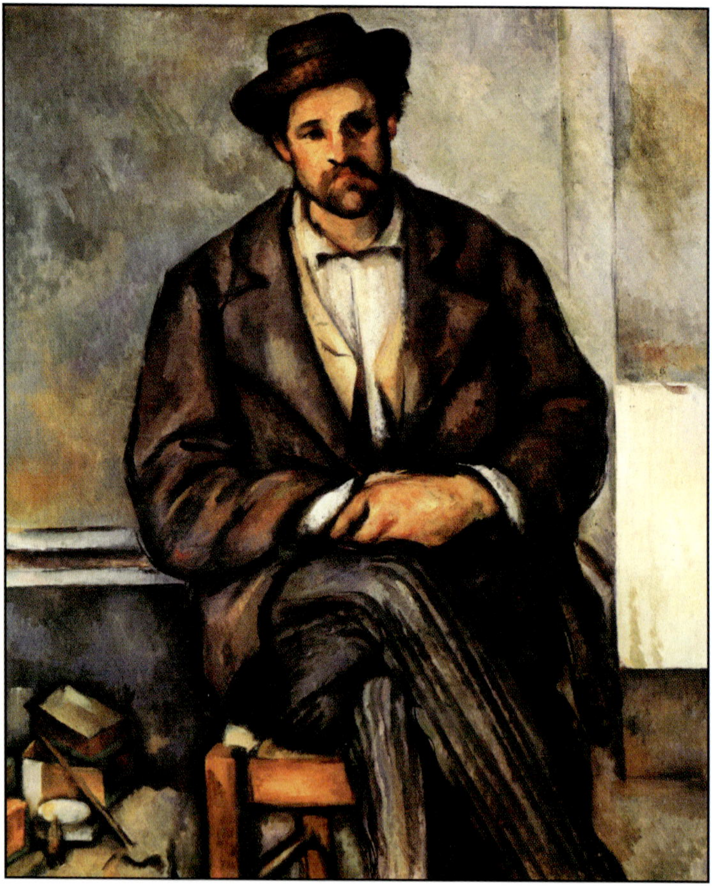

STILL LIFE WITH ORANGES

1900, Museum of Modern Art, New York
60.6 x 73.3 cm

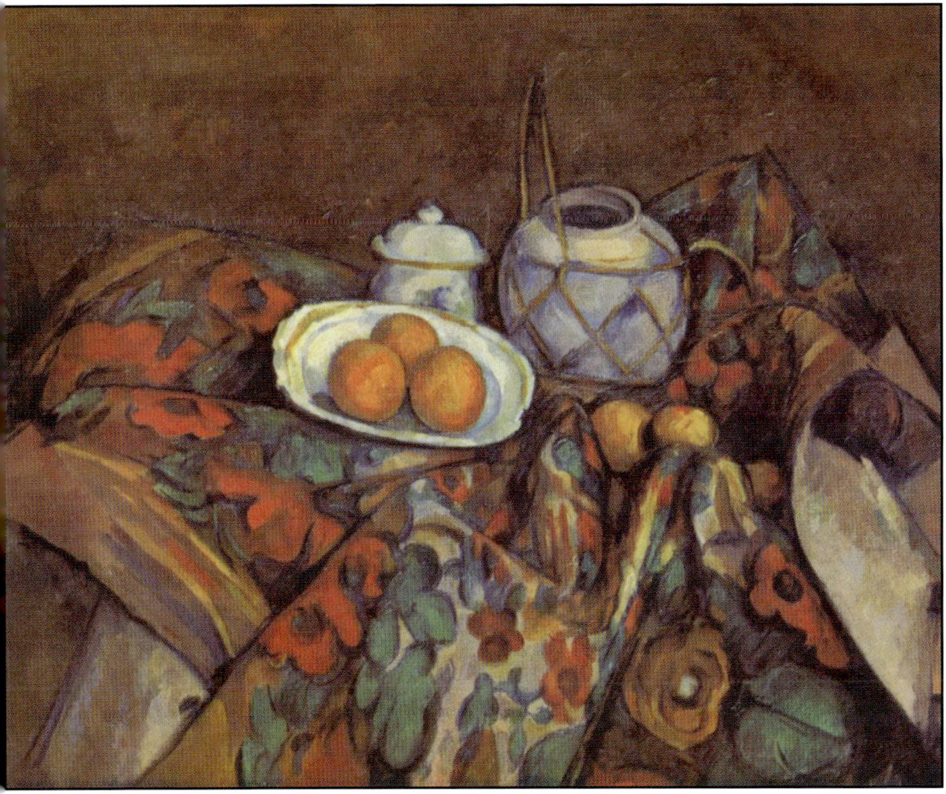

Plate 69

ROAD NEAR MONT SAINTE-VICTOIRE

1902, The State Hermitage Museum, St. Petersburg, Russia
81 x 99 cm

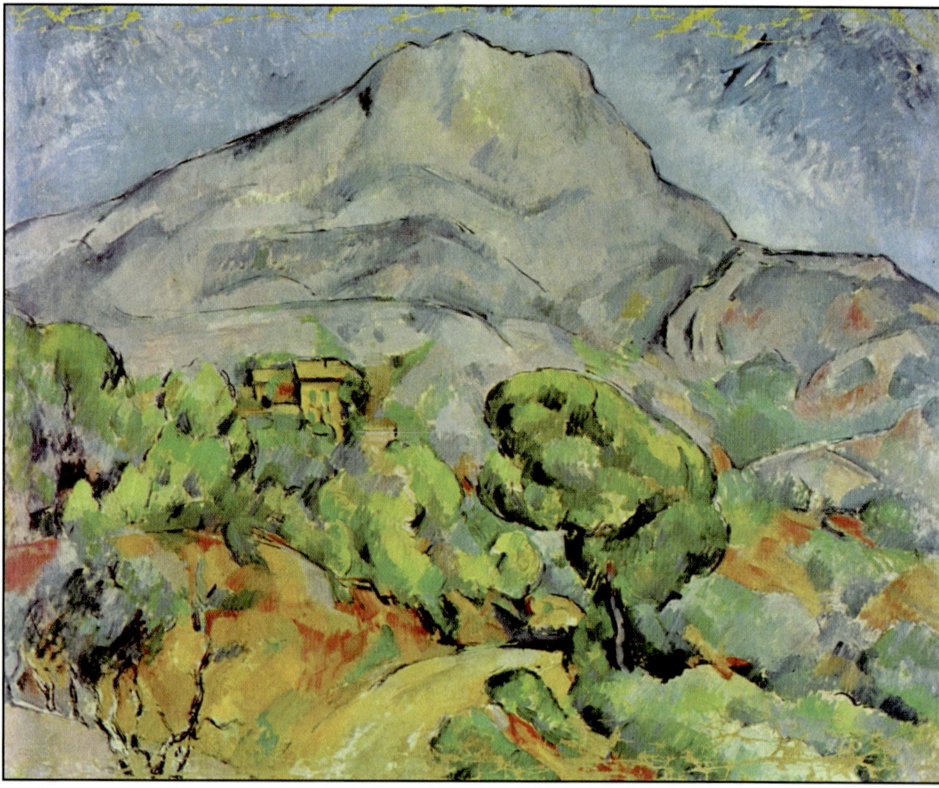

STILL LIFE: VASE WITH FLOWERS

1903, Private Collection
73 x 60 cm

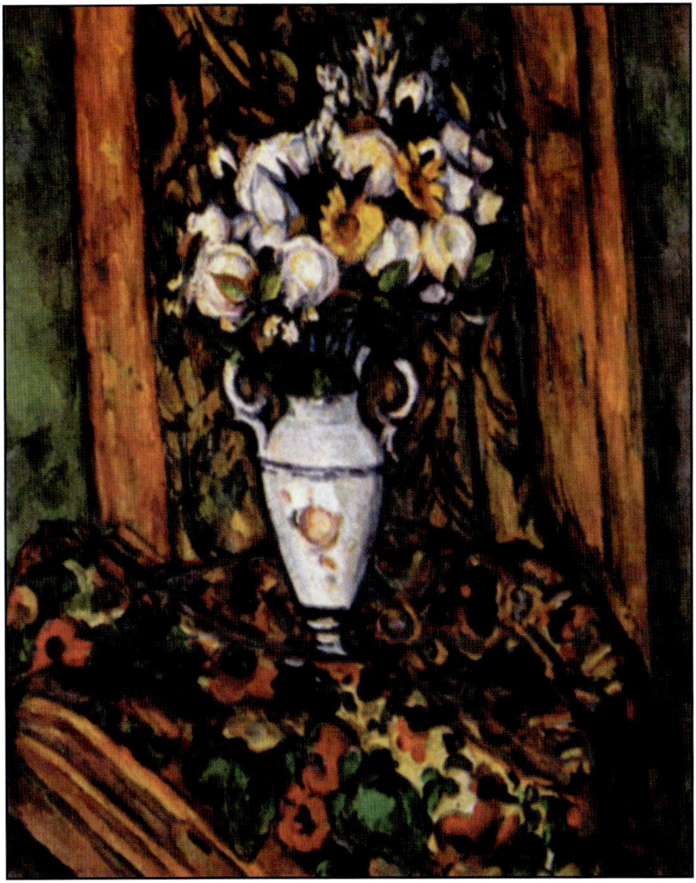

BATHERS AT REST

1904, Musée d'Orsay, Paris
22 x 33 cm

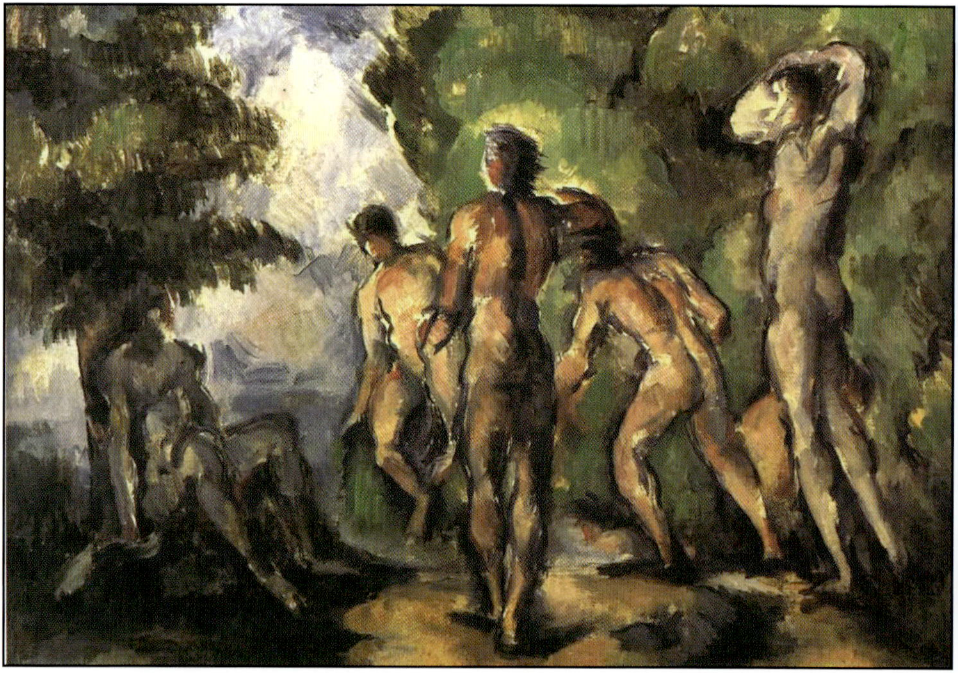

CHATEAU NOIR

1904, National Gallery of Art, Washington, DC
73.7 x 96.6 cm

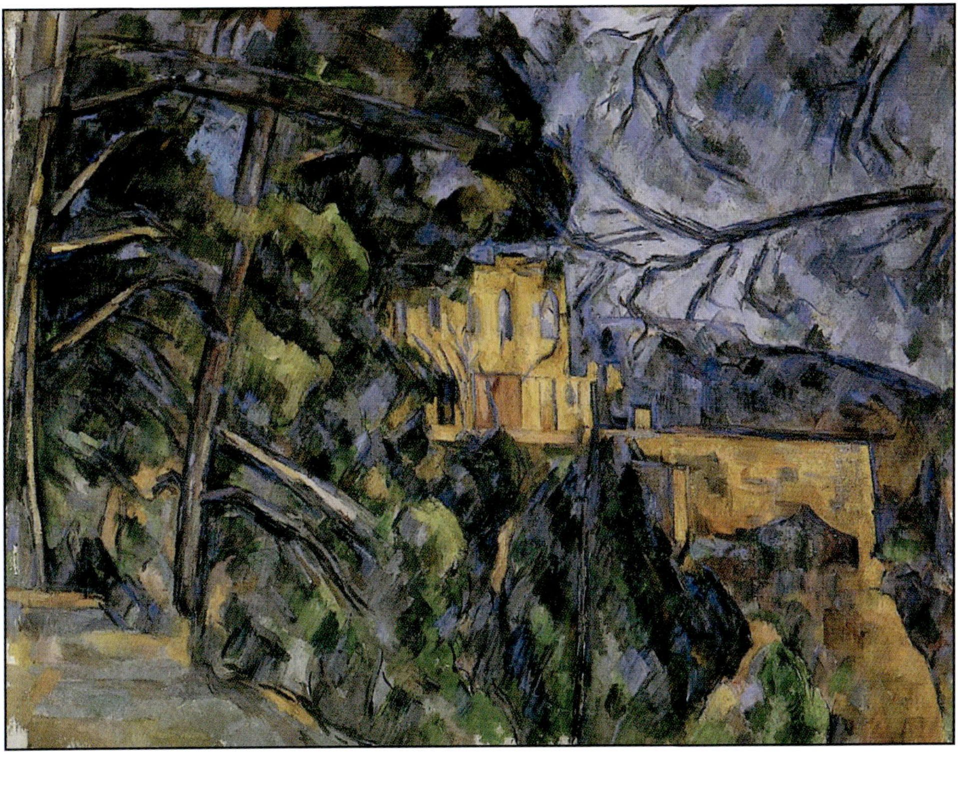

Plate 73

ROCKS NEAR THE CAVES BELOW THE CHATEAU NOIR

1904 Musée d'Orsay, Paris, France
65 x 54 cm

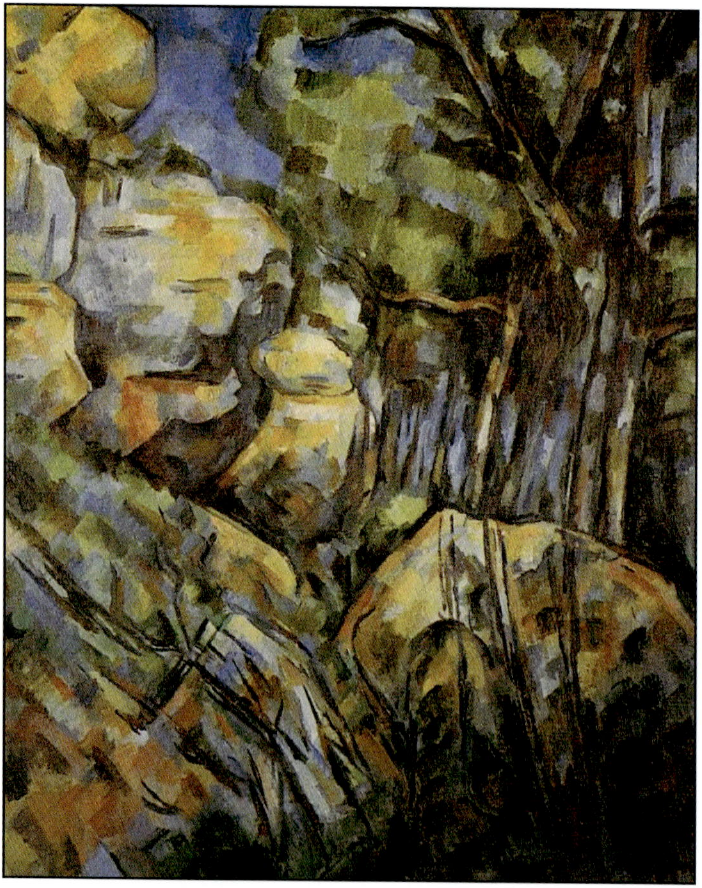

ROSES IN A BOTTLE

1904, National Gallery of Art, Washington, DC
43.6 x 31 cm

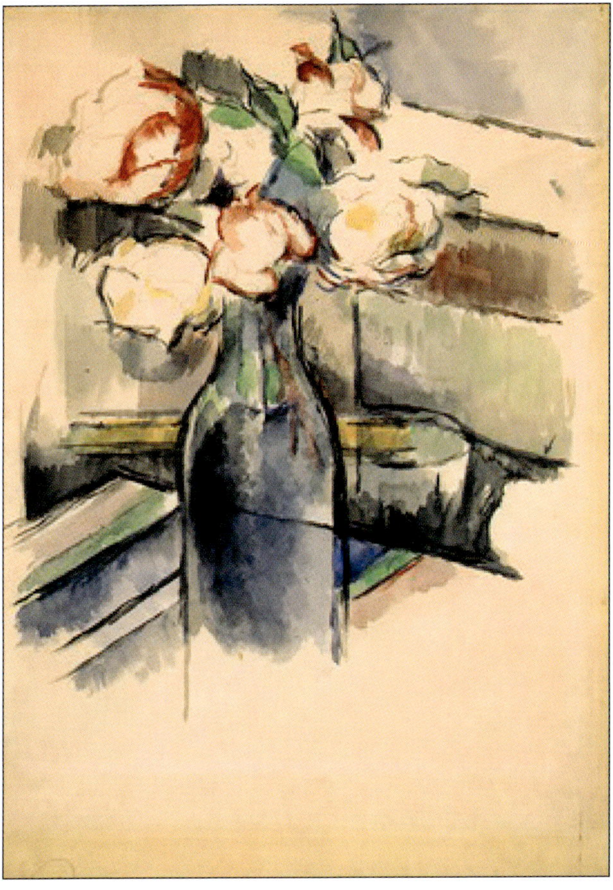

Plate 75

STILL LIFE WITH APPLES, A BOTTLE AND A MILK POT

1904 Dallas Museum of Fine Arts, Texas
48.6 x 63.2

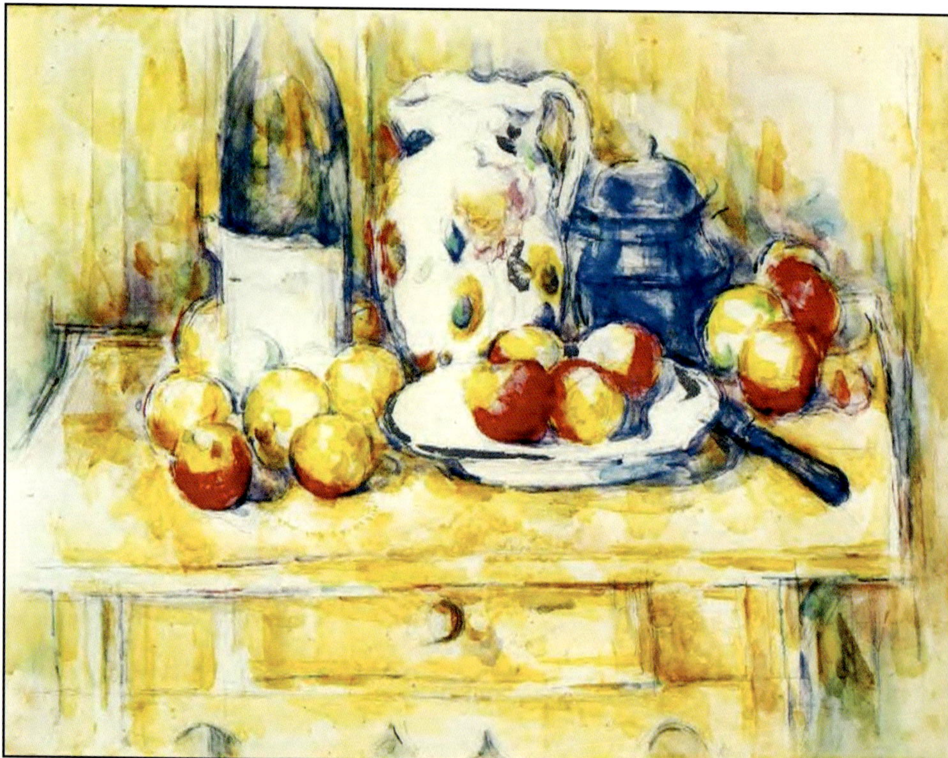

MONTAGNE SAINTE-VICTOIRE AND THE BLACK CHATEAU

1905 Bridgestone Museum of Art, Tokyo
65.6 x 81 cm

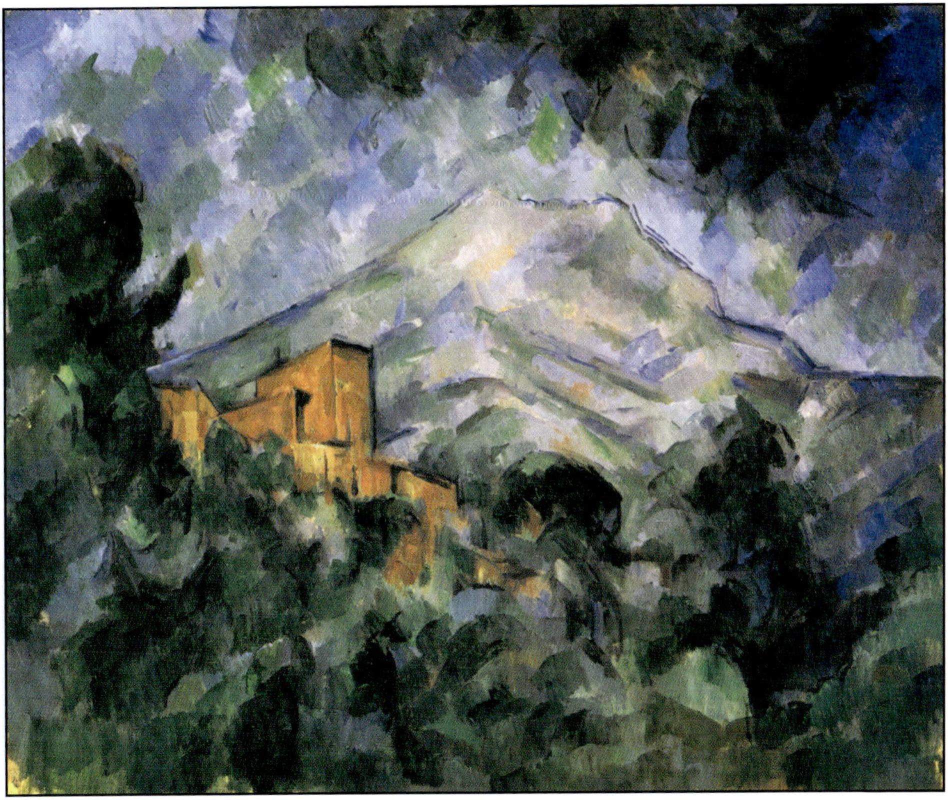

Plate 77

STILL LIFE WITH FLOWER HOLDER

1905, National Gallery of Art, Washington, DC
81.2 x 106 cm

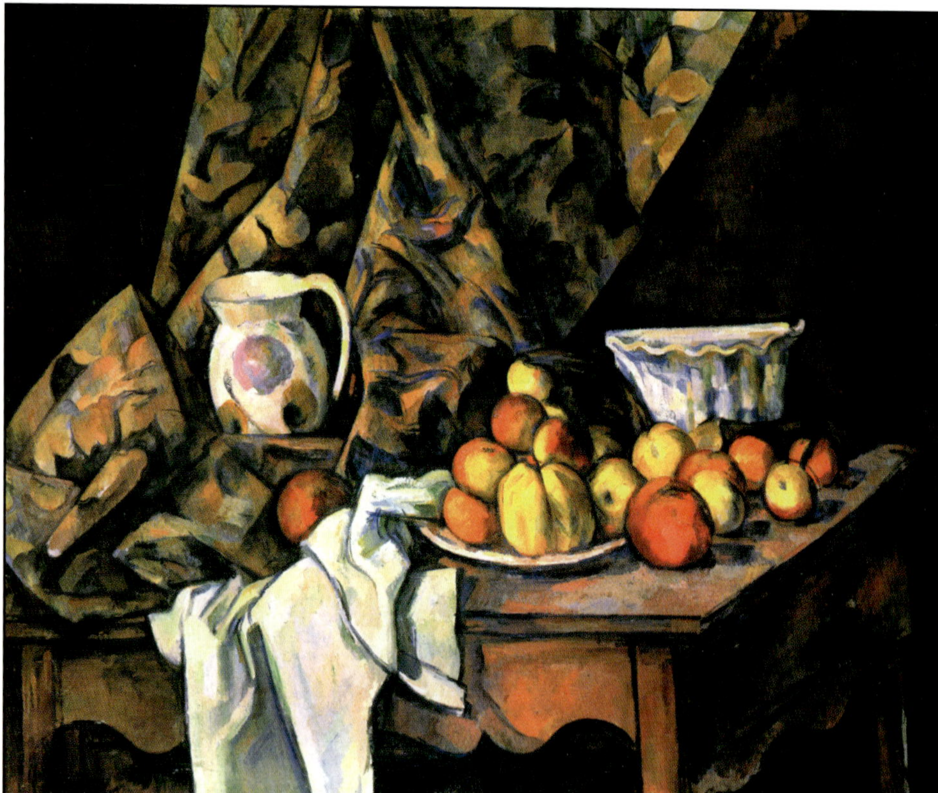

Plate 78

MAN WEARING A STRAW HAT

1905, Art Institute of Chicago
479 x 315 mm

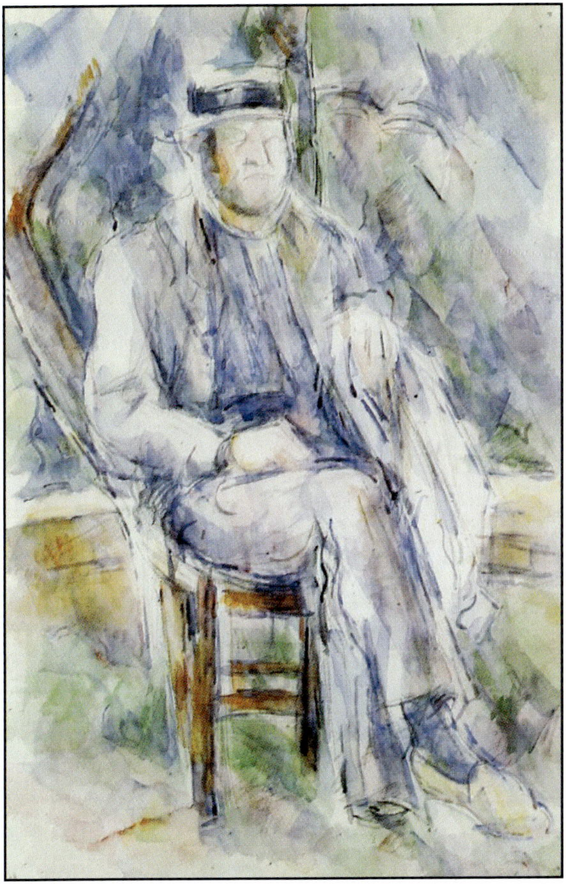

Plate 79

LARGE BATHERS II

1906, Philadelphia Museum of Art
208 x 249 cm

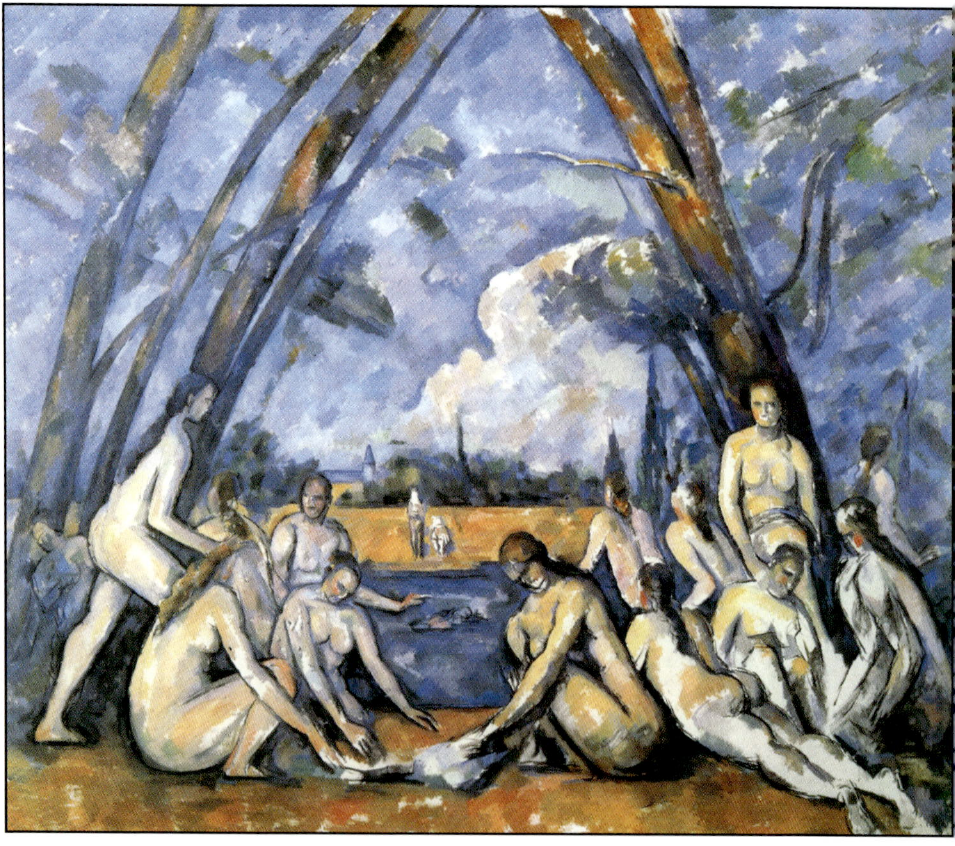

Plate 80

MONT SAINTE-VICTOIRE SEEN FROM LES LAUVES

1906, The Nelson-Atkins Museum of Art, Kansas City, Missouri
63.82 x 81.6 cm

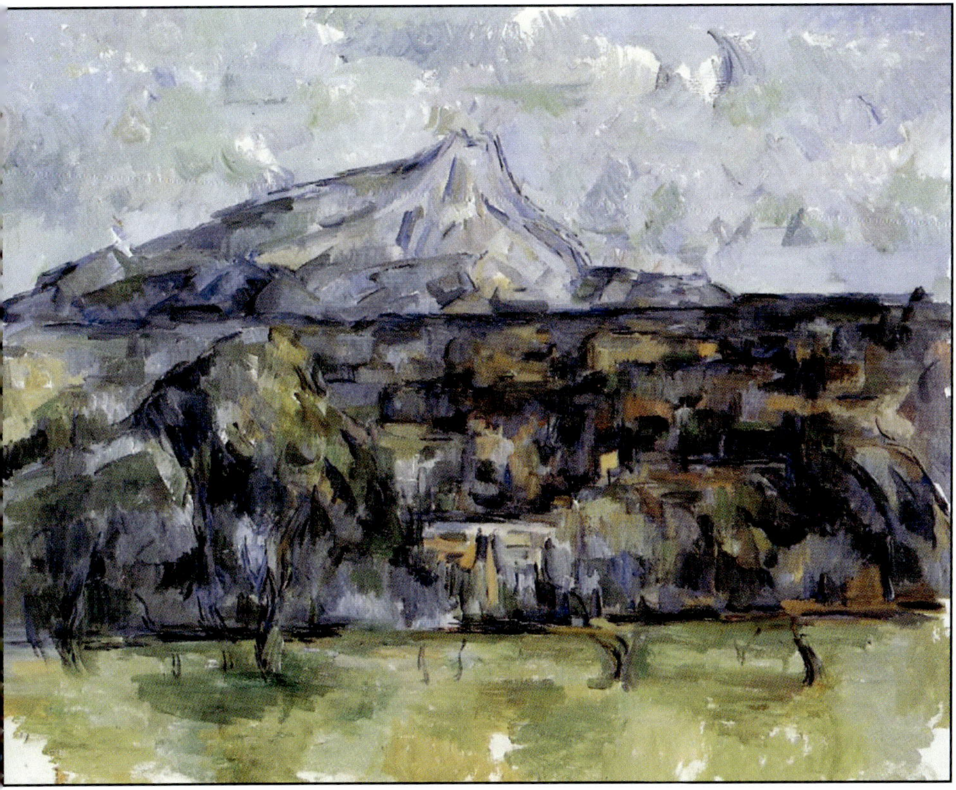

Plate 81

MORNING IN PROVENCE

1906, Albright-Knox Art Gallery, Buffalo, New York
102.87 x 85.09

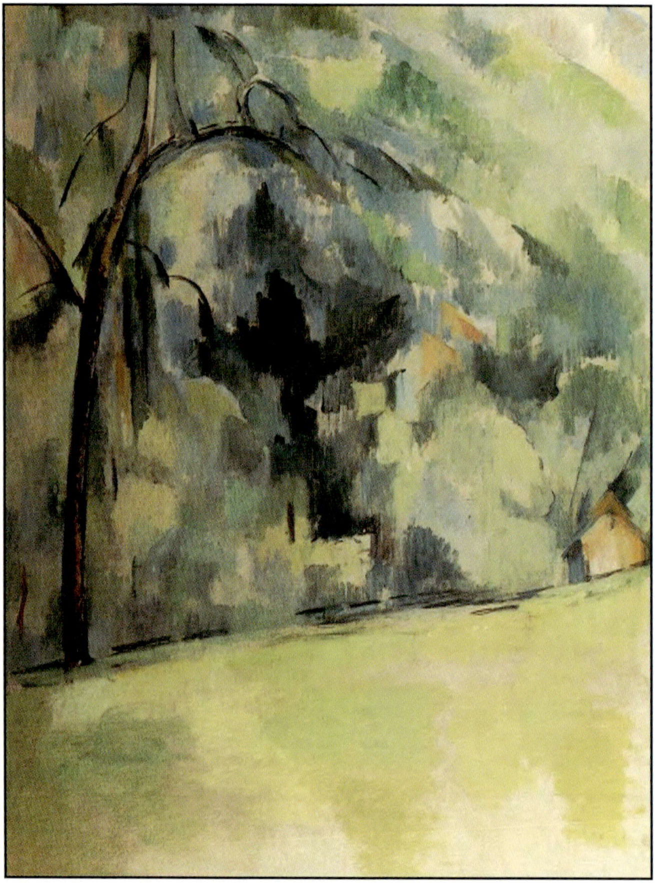

THE GARDENER VALLIER

1906, Foundation E.G. Bührle Collection, Zurich
65 x 54 cm

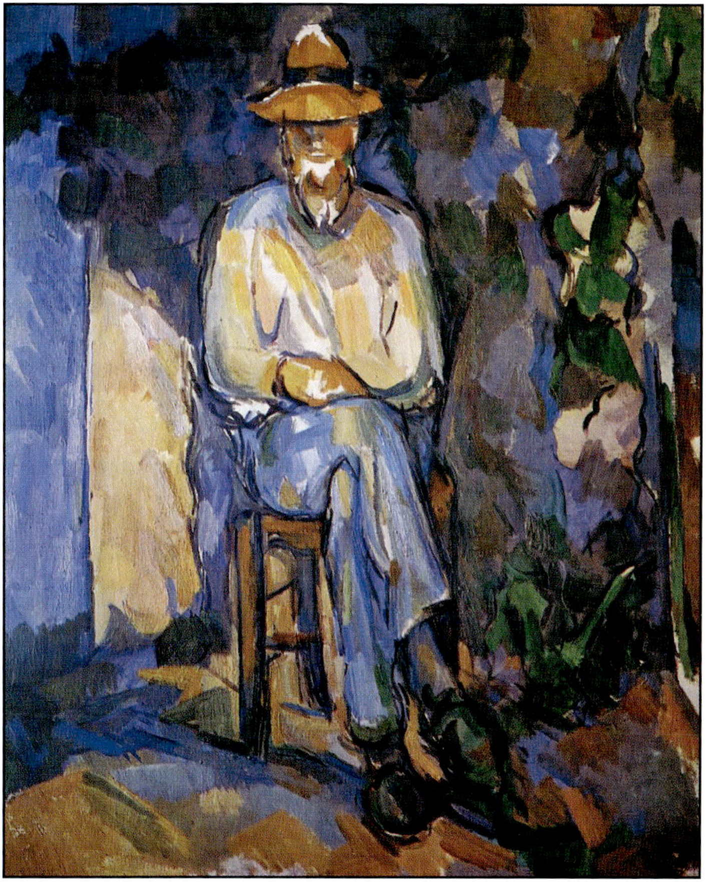

INDEX